WHY CAN'T POTATOES WALK?

Also by Lars-Åke Janzon:

How Long Can a Fly Fly?

WHY CAN'T POTATOES WALK?

200 ANSWERS TO POSSIBLE AND IMPOSSIBLE QUESTIONS ABOUT ANIMALS AND NATURE

LARS-ÅKE JANZON

TRANSLATED BY
BRANDON SCHULTZ

SKYHORSE PUBLISHING

Publisher's note: *Why Can't Potatoes Walk?* was originally published in Sweden, so readers may notice the book contains a large number of facts about animals in Scandinavia, in addition to trivia about animals around the world.

First published by Norstedts, Sweden, in 2012, as *Varför kan inte potatisar gå?* by Lars-Åke Janzon. Published by agreement with Norstedts Agency.

Designed and illustrated by Lukas Möllersten

Skyhorse Publishing books may be purchased in bulk at special discounts for sales promotion, corporate gifts, fund-raising, or educational purposes. Special editions can also be created to specifications. For details, contact the Special Sales Department, Skyhorse Publishing, 307 West 36th Street, 11th Floor, New York, NY 10018 or info@skyhorsepublishing.com.

Skyhorse® and Skyhorse Publishing® are registered trademarks of Skyhorse Publishing, Inc.®, a Delaware corporation.

www.skyhorsepublishing.com

10 9 8 7 6 5 4 3 2 1

Library of Congress Cataloging-in-Publication Data is available on file.

ISBN 978-1-62087-734-0

Printed in the United States of America

CONTENTS

INTRODUCTION

Why Can't Potatoes Walk? Why is this the title of a book about animals, large and small?

Yes, one may certainly wonder about this. When I made this book and its predecessor, *How Long Can a Fly Fly?,* I strived to inspire a curiosity about, and an understanding of, what life and evolution were—how nature had arranged these for itself. The question "why can't potatoes walk?" is related to this.

Well, why can't they?

In short, I could say because they do not need to! But of course it's a little more complicated than that. Animals and plants have developed such an incredible variety of ways to find food, procreate, protect against enemies, and so on. This natural diversity never ceases to fascinate me, and I hope to convey this fascination in my books. Hopefully, the reader also picks up a few things, more or less useful, along the way. Happy reading!

HOW THEY LOOK!

COLORS

Are zebras white with black stripes or black with white stripes?

For a long time it was thought that zebras were white with black stripes, but current embryological research shows that the opposite is true.

All zebras have a dark base that is black, brown, or beige, depending on the species. Over this dark base run white or light gray stripes, which may run together across the abdomen, creating a cohesive field of stripes. Even the tail and mane are colored, and there is a fine tuft of hair at the bottom of the tail.

It is not uncommon to find different color variations within a species. For example there are three color variations of red fox, namely, red, cross, and black.

The black fox is jet black and can appear to be a shining silver color when its topcoat is laced with white tips. The cross fox has a black band along the back and another one across the shoulders, forming a cross. And the red fox is, of course, red.

Genetic expression of these variants is determined by four different genes, which interact in various combinations. Extreme groups consist of the red and silver, while the cross fox is an intermediate form. Although not common, black foxes are quite natural.

In addition to the three basic variants, there may be different color variations in natural fox populations.

FIREFOX

One of these is that which Linnaeus called "firefox," and it has a black-tipped tail and an ashen stomach, like a red fox that walked through a fire. Linnaeus first classified this as a separate species, *Canis alopex*, but later reconsidered. In *Fauna Suecica* Linnaeus wrote: *C. vulpes ferrugineus*, which means rust- or generally dark-colored.

Other unusual color variants of foxes include a white coat with black-tipped ears or a white ring around the neck.

What color would a chameleon be on a chessboard?

One thing we can immediately conclude is that the chameleon would not be checked in black and white. There are about 80 different species of chameleon worldwide, and no species behaves exactly the same as any other. The color change, caused by contraction or expansion of microscopic pigment cells in the skin, is primarily due to light, temperature, or the animal's state of mind. Color change, therefore, does not depend on the background. In general, chameleons get brighter at higher temperatures; thus, they become lighter at night and bolder in strong light. When a chameleon is scared, it will become mostly grayish-brown. There are numerous factors that affect a chameleon's color at any given time, and each species generally has a rather limited color range.

Why are polar bears white?

Polar bears have white fur to blend in with their surroundings and, underneath, they have black skin to more effectively absorb heat. Each hair is hollow to provide optimum insulation against cold. (This is believed to be the reason that the coat looks black when photographed with ultraviolet light. UV light is evidently absorbed by the hollow strands. This effect also may make the coat appear yellowish.) The hair conducts

heat radiation to the black skin and helps the animal to absorb as much heat as possible. Add a 4-inch layer of pure fat and you will understand how polar bears keep from freezing. In fact, they must move slowly to prevent overheating in the Arctic, where the temperature does not exceed 50°F in the summer and drops to −40°F in the winter. In contrast to many other animals, the polar bear's fur does not change in the summer, but remains thick and white year round.

THE CLIMATE IS THREATENING THE POLAR BEAR

Rising temperatures forced many animals to draw closer to the north and south poles. As the temperature rises, it melts a greater part of their natural habitats away. There are two major threats to polar bears that are directly caused by climate change. First, their hunting grounds disappear as the ice melts; they depend on ice for accessing their food. With the help of its excellent sense of smell and excellent underwater vision, the polar bear hunts among floes on the shores. It can wait for hours at one of the seals' breathing holes. When the seal surfaces, the bear strikes. It kills the seal with a single bite of the head or with a blow from its massive, heavy frame. The polar bear depends on ice to hunt. In summer, when the ice pulls north, the polar bear must set off hundreds of miles to get food. The second threat comes when the ice disappears and the polar bear is unable to swim back to shore and drowns. And polar bears can swim far. They have been seen swimming 100 miles from land!

POLAR BEAR FACTS

The polar bear has a second, transparent eyelid (nictitating membrane) that acts as a pair of swimming goggles and protects its eyes while swimming.

The bear's maximum speed when running on land is about 30 miles per hour. Its walking speed is about 3 miles per hour.

A polar bear can live to be 25–30 years old in the wild, and about 40 years old in captivity.

Unlike other bears, polar bears are not naturally afraid of humans. If they are very hungry, they will attack us.

Some polar bears hibernate in snow caves, while others are active year round. Pregnant females always dig down in a cave to hibernate (October–April).

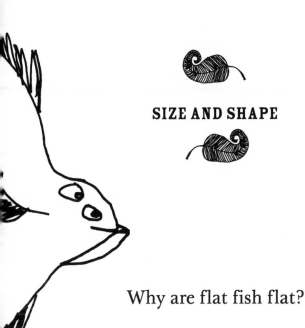

SIZE AND SHAPE

Why are flat fish flat?

There are several different kinds of "flat" fish. Rays have become flat probably as a combined result of their food being on the ground, their mouths facing downward, and their need to bury themselves for protection. The free-swimming mantas probably have bottom-dwelling ancestors.

As regards the so-called flatfish, there is a theory that states that they are flat because the fry (young fish) is so heavy that it sinks to the bottom, resulting in the second eye having moved to the face-up side—the side that was not down in the sand. To me, this sounds more like an ex post construction. Alternatively, one can speculate whether a behavior that is present in another fish may have been the cause. This fish lies on its side on the sandy bottom and plays dead. When another

19

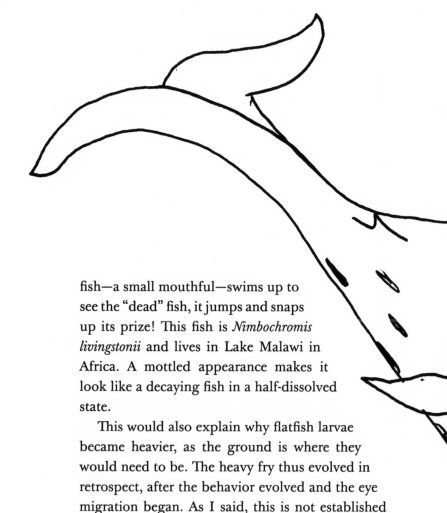

fish—a small mouthful—swims up to
see the "dead" fish, it jumps and snaps
up its prize! This fish is *Nimbochromis
livingstonii* and lives in Lake Malawi in
Africa. A mottled appearance makes it
look like a decaying fish in a half-dissolved
state.

This would also explain why flatfish larvae
became heavier, as the ground is where they
would need to be. The heavy fry thus evolved in
retrospect, after the behavior evolved and the eye
migration began. As I said, this is not established
truth, but still . . .

20

Why are blue whales so big?

It is certainly an advantage to be enormous when you live in a cold environment. Whales live, as we know, in the water, where heat is lost much faster than on land (think of how much quicker you begin to freeze in water that is 68°F than on land when the air temperature is 68°F!). As if that were not enough, the blue whale developed a migration pattern in which it migrates to the polar regions, where it is extremely cold, to eat. Large animals lose less heat because the ratio of surface (skin) to volume (body) is small—body heat radiates out through the skin. Thanks to its size,

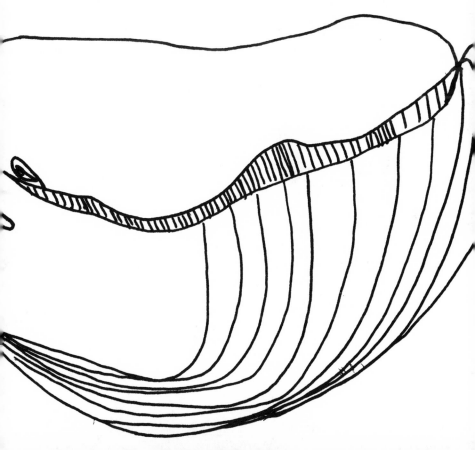

the blue whale can spend less energy on maintaining body heat. Whales are also special in that they have extra insulation (blubber) to cover them and keep them warm. Blubber also serves as a food supply during the winter months when they are in the warmer waters to mate and give birth to cubs, and where food is not nearly as plentiful.

Another benefit of being enormous is that the risk of being killed by a predator is lower (but, unfortunately, this has not applied with humans, who have made the whales almost extinct in their search of the whales' coveted oil).

Undeniably, it can also be an advantage to be large when it comes to fighting and to finding a partner, but we know very little about this when it comes to blue whales.

Since it is important for animals to produce offspring as soon as possible, the early whales that grew the most quickly probably benefited in this area, leading the species to become larger.

Did you know that . . .

. . . every day a blue whale poops 3 percent of its weight? That's over 5 tons a day!

. . . the blue whale is the animal with the largest heart, while the sperm whale is considered to have the largest brain?

A prerequisite for the blue whale and other large whales to develop was that there was plenty of food available. Belonging to this family are the baleen whales—that is to say, those that evolution equipped with a new kind of feeding apparatus, baleen (instead of teeth), with which they can filter large amounts of krill and other food from large volumes of water. By starting to migrate to the polar regions, where krill and other species exist in huge quantities, they were given access to a very rich food source, as there was less competition.

THEORIES OF BEACHED WHALES

The reasons that individual whales or entire pods become stranded are unclear, and frequently debated. One possibility is that one whale, perhaps the dominant whale, simply loses its orientation and swims off in the wrong direction. The other whales in the pack then follow because they are inclined to follow the choices of their leader.

Another theory is that the whales that reside in deep water react to the so-called rush when they feel the seabed against their abdomens, which could lead them to land.

None of these explanations is particularly convincing. Therefore, it has more recently been accepted that the different sounds that are on the same wavelength as a whale's own communication (underwater explosions, ship machinery, or sonar) could be interfering with the whale's orientation. There are observations that could indicate that this is the case, but it has yet to be proven. Still, after major naval exercises where sonar was used, mass-stranding of whales has been observed.

Which is tallest—the giraffe or the blue whale?

It is a bit difficult to find the dimensions of exactly how tall a blue whale is, but it's still easy to crown a victor. The blue whale, with its near-100-foot length, is easily the longest, but tallest it is not. A blue whale is estimated to be between 10 and 12 feet high, while a giraffe can be nearly 20 feet tall.

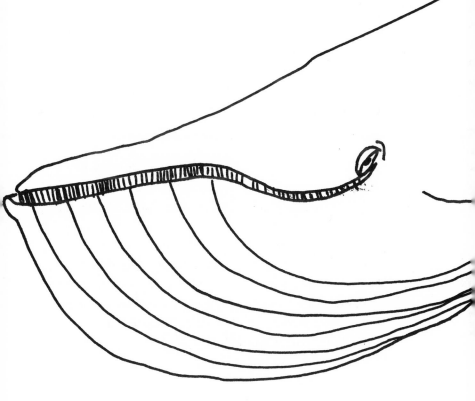

THE LARGEST AND SMALLEST AMONG MAMMALS

The largest and heaviest mammal is the blue whale, *Balaenoptera musculus*. The length of an adult blue whale is a maximum of about 108 feet, with a corresponding weight of just over 180 tons. The whales in the southern hemisphere are larger than those in the northern hemisphere.

The largest land mammal is the African savannah elephant, *Loxodonta africana*. Males are larger than females. They can live to be 70 years old and they continue to grow throughout life. They can grow up to 13 feet tall (at the shoulders) and can weigh up to 7 tons.

The smallest sea mammal is Commerson's dolphin, *Cephalorhynchus commersonii*. Commerson's dolphins range in length from 4 to 5.5 feet and can weigh up to 19 pounds.

On land, the smallest are likely the shrews of the genera *Sorex*, *Microsorex*, and *Suncus*, with possibly the white-toothed pygmy shrew, *Suncus etruscus* (Etruscan pygmy shrew), or the lesser pygmy mouse, *Sorex minutissimus*, being the absolute smallest. Kitti's hog-nosed bat (or bumblebee bat), *Craseonycteris thonglongyai*, is also very small, with a size close to that of a bumblebee.

Penguins

Penguins vary dramatically in size and weight, although they are all quite similar in body shape and appearance. They are usually blue-black or blue-gray on the top, while the underside is white. Penguins have a dense plumage that consists of three layers of short feathers. They have a streamlined body, and wings are reduced to strong, narrow, and rigid "fins" with which they can move through the water at high speed. Their feet and legs are short and sharp, and their legs are placed far back on the body. When penguins swim, they use their tail feathers like rudders. Features that distinguish one species from another—tufts, lines, bands, or other markings—are usually on the head and upper chest. Under the chest is usually plain gray or brown.

A LAYER OF FAT DOES THE TRICK

Penguins are primarily adapted to live in a cool climate; they can exist in tropical regions, but only in connection with the cold ocean currents (such as the Humboldt Current or the Benguela and Agulhas Currents). To keep warm in a cold environment, penguins have a very thick, dense, and waterproof plumage. Moreover, they have a proper fat layer inside the skin, and a system of blood vessels acts as a kind of heat-exchanger in the legs and the wings.

. . . most penguin litters consist of two eggs? Only the emperor penguin and king penguin lay a single egg. Incubation is 32–63 days, depending on the species. The egg is kept at a temperature of 102°F in the skin flap, although the ambient temperature may be −40°F with wind blowing at a velocity of 90 miles per hour.

. . . male king penguins have the ability to store food in their stomachs for up to three weeks? Since the males sometimes brood the eggs for many days before the females take over, they have developed the ability to store food for a long time while keeping it fairly fresh.

. . . emperor penguins can dive down to a depth of over 1,800 feet and stay underwater for up to 20 minutes?

. . . typical penguins swim at speeds of 3–6 miles per hour, and stay underwater for an average of 2.5 minutes, but can be underwater for up to 5 minutes?

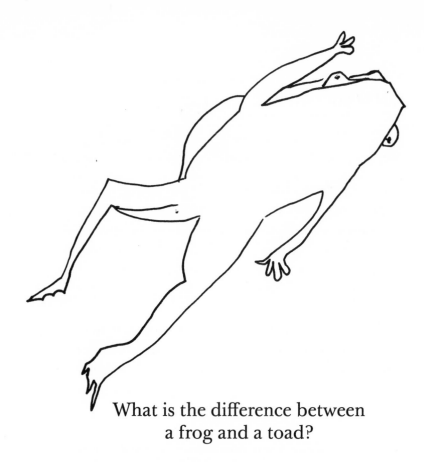

What is the difference between a frog and a toad?

The species in the order of anurans, *Anura*, are called either frogs or toads.

TOADS
are characterized by warty skin with many poison glands and a stocky body with short legs

FROGS
generally have smooth skin and slender bodies

move awkwardly and are not good at jumping

are relatively flexible and good at jumping

Toads and other amphibians have a difficult life in environments near cities. Allowing parts of a garden to grow a little wilder creates places where toads can roam. Toads eat worms, snails, and ants. In addition, they gladly feast on mosquitoes and other night-flying insects that are attracted to light sources.

TIPS

A small garden lantern on the ground—preferably with a light flat stone over it—could become an excellent smorgasbord for toads. Additionally, an accessible compost pile is an ideal wintering place for these animals.

And while you're at it, an undisturbed pile of twigs is an excellent wintering spot for hedgehogs, and they also like it when you allow the garden to grow a little wild.

Did you know that...

. . . a bee walks by moving the first and third legs on one side of the body simultaneously with the second leg of the other side? This means that the middle legs are never used together. This mechanism is true of nearly all insects—that is, all six-legged creatures.

. . . the edible snail is actually born with a small shell house, a "mini house," which it then carries through life? In the shell, you can see different numbers of calcium lines that tell the snail's age. Each line corresponds to one year. The edible snail generally lives 8–10 years, but specimens up to 37 years old have been found.

. . . an earthworm can be over 10 years old? But in the wild it is usually not more than 2 years old.

. . . leeches only need to eat (i.e., drink blood) once a year? But when they eat, they eat quite a bit. They suck in an amount of blood equivalent to 5–10 times their own weight!

. . . there are over 60 species of ladybugs in Sweden alone? Worldwide, there are around 5,000 different species of ladybugs.

. . . the moth with the largest wingspan is the nocturnal *Thysania agrippina*? The largest known specimen measured 12 inches (more than the height of a standard piece of paper). This moth can be found from Brazil to the southern United States.

. . . the moth with the largest wing surface in the world is the Hercules moth, *Coscinocera hercules*? The largest known specimen has a wing area of over 100 square inches (larger than a standard sheet of paper). Hercules moths are found in tropical Australia and New Guinea.

. . . of all the world's birds, the magnificent frigatebird has the largest wing surface relative to body weight? All birds have very light bones, but frigatebird bones are extraordinarily light.

How long can a viper get?

The Swedish record held by a viper was from Härjedalen (Kappruet) and is 41 inches, which is very unusual. The general rule in Sweden would be that a female viper would not exceed 31 inches, and a male 30 inches, but even these lengths are now rare.

→ Monotremes are the only mammals that lay eggs. Typical mammalian traits of monotremes are that they have fur, they have three ossicles in the middle ear, and they have a single bone in the lower jaw.

→ Today's monotremes consist of two families with a total of three genera and five species.

→ The platypus, *Ornithorhynchus anatinus*, is the only member of the family Ornithorhynchidae.

→ The echidna family, Tachyglossidae, consists of two genera: short-beaked echidnas, *Tachyglossus*, with one species, and long-beaked echidnas, *Zaglossus*, with three species.

→ Monotremes have a well-developed diaphragm muscle.

→ Monotremes maintain a constant body temperature (albeit lower than that of other mammals).

→ Female monotremes produce milk in the mammary glands as food for their offspring.

Why did the beaver's tail get so big?

The beaver's tail has several uses. One is to warn other beavers of danger. It makes a loud bang when it smacks the surface and sounds much like when you slap the surface of water with an oar.

Mostly, the tail just hangs behind the beaver as it swims, but it can also be used to get some extra speed when kicking with the hind legs is not enough. The tail is also used to steer, much like a rudder on a sailboat.

BEAVER FACTS

The beaver is Sweden's largest rodent. It grows to about 27–39 inches long (the tail adds a further 12–16 inches) and weighs as much as 40–45 pounds. A beaver typically lives to be at least 10–15 years old, and sometimes even up to 30 years. Because it is aquatic and nocturnal, it is difficult to spot; usually bite marks on gnawed trees are the best indication that a beaver has been there. Since the large front teeth grow continuously, the beaver needs to gnaw to grind them down.

The beaver lives mainly in freshwater but also in brackish water. It must have access to fresh water, both to drink and to wash away salt from its coat, which otherwise destroys its insulating ability.

In both sexes, special secretions are stored in two abdominal sacs, called castor sacs. Urine drains into the castor sacs and undergoes a chemical process, becoming a concentrate called castoreum, and slowly releases a scent. The beaver uses this mucus for territorial marking.

In the 1300s and 1400s beavers were common in Sweden. By the mid-1700s they had become rare, and by the end of the 1800s they were completely eradicated from the country.

In 1920 a few beavers were released in Bjurälven in Jämtland. This successful introduction was followed by a few more releases. From these individuals, the beavers have now recovered and spread to most parts of Sweden.

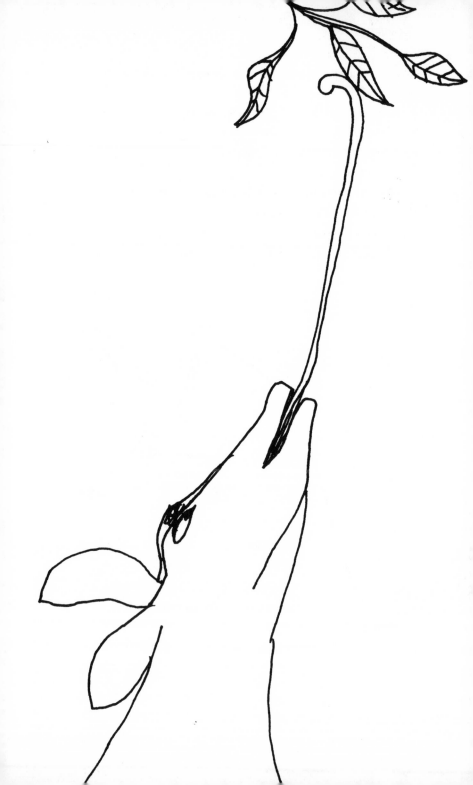

EAR, NOSE, AND THROAT

Which animal has the longest tongue?

That would be one of the giraffids, the okapi and the giraffe. The giraffe has a tongue with an average length of approximately 18 inches, while an okapi has a tongue that can be up to 20 inches long.

The giraffe has, as we know, not only a long tongue, but also a rather long neck. It can be more than 11 feet long. Such a long neck creates some special requirements for oxygen uptake. The giraffe's lungs are eight times larger than those of the human, but the respiratory rate is only one-third of ours. Slow inhalation is necessary to replace the large volume of air contained in the lungs. When the giraffe takes a new breath of fresh air, the exhaled air is not yet completely dissipated. Still, the giraffe seems to manage this problem well, even if there is a small amount of "old" air left.

The giraffe has seven neck vertebrae, just like us, but they are prolonged in giraffes.

When the giraffe bends down, there would be dramatic changes in blood pressure if not for valves that prevent blood from flowing into the head.

GIRAFFE FACTS

The giraffe is the world's tallest land animal, and the male grows to about 16 feet tall from foot to head. At the shoulders, it is about 10 feet tall.

The giraffe's front legs are longer than its back legs. It can pace slowly and can reach a very high speed. For long distances, the giraffe can reach up to 9 miles per hour, and for short distances it can reach a maximum speed of 35 miles per hour.

The Romans believed that the giraffe was a mix of leopard and camel! If you consider

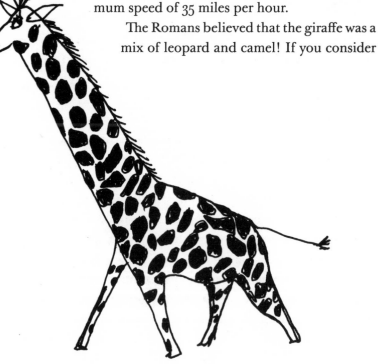

the giraffe's size and its mottled appearance, you can understand why they thought this. Linnaeus probably thought this, too, because he gave the giraffe the species name *camelopardalis*. (The species is the second part of the scientific name.)

The name giraffe is derived from the Arabic *zarafa*, which means "sweet" or "lovable."

Giraffes live alone or in small flocks. They communicate in a frequency inaudible to humans, below 20 Hertz—the so-called infrasonic zone.

Chameleons have an even longer tongue in relation to body length. The same goes for the pangolin, which is said to have a tongue corresponding to half its body length. Pangolins (several species) vary in length from 12 inches to 35 inches.

DARWIN PREDICTED A LONG TONGUE. Darwin's star, *Angraecum sesquipedale*, is an orchid that grows in Madagascar. It grows as an epiphyte (i.e., a plant that lives on another plant without taking nourishment from it) in tropical forests from sea level up to 3,300 feet. The approximately 8-inch-wide flower has a 12- to 14-inch-long spur where the nectar is produced and stored. The plant was collected for the first time in 1822 and later was made famous by Charles Darwin, who predicted that the orchid pollinator must be a moth with a long proboscis to reach down into the bottom of the spur. Much later, after Darwin's death, the pollinator was discovered: a nocturnal moth with a 10-inch proboscis. The moth, which had been previously unknown to science, was named *Xanthopan morganii praedicta*, where *praedicta* means "predicted."

Did you know that...

... the bare, fleshy skin flaps over the beak of some poultry (e.g., chickens and turkeys) are called wattles or, more colloquially, bibs?

... the folds of skin that hang down between the neck and breast on moose and some cattle are called dewlaps?

Why do lynx have ear tufts?

Like domestic cats, lynx use body language to communicate with each other. On the back of the lynx's ear is a light area with a black border. The black edges lead to a black tuft on each ear. The tufts, in turn, make the ears appear larger and more visible, and they make ear movements more clear, making it easier for other lynx to interpret the movements. The same goes for the tail, which is black at the tip. The black tips are easily seen and make lynx signals clear to one another.

Did you know that...

... lynx have incredibly good hearing? A whistle that a dog can hear 1.9 miles away can be heard by a lynx from 2.8 miles! And it can hear reindeer digging for lichen in snow 1,000 feet away.

Do fish spit?

Yes, fish have saliva in terms of a lubricant and transport medium, although it is not nearly as fluid as ours.

The fish's mouth has several "glands" with different functions, but fish mouths are rinsed continuously as they breathe through their gills. Some of the substances found in human saliva are lacking in fish mouths, and are found only in the throat and stomach, where they are protected from being washed away.

However, fish, like humans, need a lubricant in the oral cavity, and theirs is rather like a smooth, thin mucus layer. The layer also serves as a transport medium for a range of substances, but does not "rinse" the entire oral cavity as it does with us; rather, it works more locally.

BIOLUMINESCENCE

Why are nocturnal insects drawn to light?

One explanation could be that moths and other nocturnal insects have navigated by starlight for thousands of years. Additionally, moths perceive ultraviolet light (which has a shorter wavelength than visible light), but we humans do not. It was not so very long ago that man invented artificial light, and the night-flying insects are also attracted to this. They have not yet "learned" to avoid or ignore it.

The more UV light emitted by a source, the more the insects are attracted to it. The problem for the nocturnal insects is that the man-made light sources are not infinitely far away, like stars, but are within their reach. When they get too close to the light source, they become confused, perhaps almost blind, and do not really know where to go.

The nocturnal insects that are attracted to light are moths, caddisflies, mayflies, Neuroptera, some parasitic wasps, predatory hornets, and some aquatic beetles, but also the occasional aquatic bird, such as the water rail.

How does a firefly work?

Most fireflies emit light from a yellow spot in the rear, under the carapace. The light is reddish when it flies, while it is yellow-green when not in motion. When many fireflies are congregated together, in a tree for example, they can flash together in time.

A clarification of fireflies and glowworms: both glowworms (Lampyridae) and fireflies (Elateridae, Pyrophorinae) are beetles, not worms or flies. In Sweden there are only two species of glowworms.

In nature there are many living creatures that glow: insects, fish, mushrooms, protozoa, cnidarians, cteno-phores, molluscs, crustaceans, acorn worms, sea squirts, ring worms, and bacteria, for example.

. . . the flashlight fish shines on its prey with a kind of headlight?

. . . the anglerfish, which lives deep in the ocean, has a huge mouth? And between the eyes, it has a "fishing rod," with a bright little tip that looks like a fish at the end? It "fishes" to attract prey.

NEON STUMP

If you think you have seen a glowing stump, it was probably a fungus called honey fungus, which is the most famous bioluminescent fungus. Fungal mycelium grows 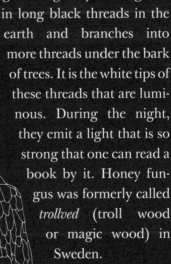 in long black threads in the earth and branches into more threads under the bark of trees. It is the white tips of these threads that are luminous. During the night, they emit a light that is so strong that one can read a book by it. Honey fungus was formerly called *trollved* (troll wood or magic wood) in Sweden.

Do dogs see in black and white?

Mammals in general have color vision, but it is worse than most other vertebrates. The quality of color vision is determined by how many different types of cones (light-sensitive cells responsible for color vision) are in the retina. Humans and other great apes have three types of cones (most sensitive to blue, green, and red), while most other mammals (including dogs and horses) have two types (most sensitive to blue and green). With only two types, one cannot distinguish as many different shades of color, but there is still color vision. With our three types of cones, we can distinguish between about half a million different color shades. Horses and dogs can distinguish only one-tenth as many, and they are especially bad at distinguishing red and orange hues. But they can easily distinguish plain green from plain red.

❖ MYTH ❖

It is a myth that bulls cannot see red, in the literal sense. Cattle, including bulls, as well as horses and dogs can distinguish an estimated one-tenth as many colors as humans, and they are especially bad at distinguishing red and orange hues. But they can easily distinguish plain green from plain red. Whether it is the color red that makes them *see red* when faced with a matador is a completely different issue.

50

Did you know that...

. . . the Philippine tarsier, *Tarsius syrichta*, has the largest eyes in proportion to body size? Each eye is so large that it would be the size of a grapefruit on a human face.

. . . the giant squid, *Architeuthis dux*, has the largest eyes of any animal? In 1878, in the Thimble Tickle Bay in Canada, a specimen was found that had eyes that were nearly 16 inches in diameter.

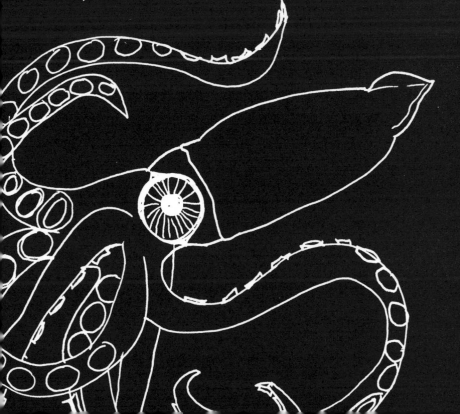

HOW THEY ACT!

SNAKE SEX AND CHASTITY BELTS

How do sea urchins mate?

All echinoderms (including sea urchins) are broadcast reproducers, which means that the male and female do not need to join together for the eggs to be fertilized. When sea urchins reproduce, the eggs and sperm are released into the water; thus, the eggs are fertilized.

The sea urchin's fertilization method is called external fertilization. The same method is used by most of the fish species. In other words, the roe (eggs) are released into the water outside the female's body and land on plants or the sea bottom, and then the male releases his milt (sperm) over them. Among the more than 32,000 species of fish, reproduction habits vary greatly. Some species, such as the three-spined stickleback, *Gasterosteus aculeatus*, guard the roe and fry (young), while with others, such as the mouthbreeders of the Cichlidae family, some guard the roe, and others guard only the hatched fry. In the vast majority, however, none of the fry can survive on their own.

Those that do not practice external fertilization use internal fertilization (i.e., the male injects sperm into the female).

In these species, eggs develop in the female and are nourished from the yolk, but in some, such as some sharks, the eggs do not develop embryos, but are nourished directly from the mother's body. In both cases, babies are born alive—these species are live-bearers.

Examples of live-bearing fish families:
Anablepidae: four-eyed fish
Goodeidae: highland carp
Hemiramphidae: halfbeaks
Potamotrygonidae: stingrays
Embiotocidae: live-bearing surfperch

There are fish that give birth to live young in all of the world's oceans and freshwater areas, including both the polar regions and the temperate regions.

In ovoviviparous fish, such as wobbegong sharks, *Orectolobus* spp., developed eggs are protected inside the female's body, but they do not take nutrients from the female. The egg lives on its store of yolk (and egg white, if available). Sometimes the eggs hatch inside the female, in which cases the young are born alive. In others, eggs hatch immediately after laying. Ovoviviparity occurs in many animal groups, including insects, snails, fish, and snakes.

Viviparity means that an egg develops into an embryo via the placenta, which takes nutrients from the mother. Viviparity has been developed by several groups of animals independently. We mammals are obviously viviparous, except the monotremes. In fish, many sharks are viviparous, such as the hammerhead shark and the gray shark.

Another strange (or rather, unusual—in nature nothing is really strange) method is exhibited by the octopus. The male produces sperm that is contained in special packets called spermatophores. At mating time, one of the male's arms is converted to enter the female and transfer these packets to her. Through this arm—called a hectocotylus—the male empties the sperm packets into the female's mantle cavity. The packet walls are destroyed, and the sperm is stored until needed for fertilization, when the female then lays the eggs.

Did you know that...

... hedgehogs mate like most mammals, despite the quills? The male climbs up on the female's back and, during mating, the female presses her body against the ground while keeping the quills down, close to her body.

What does hermaphrodite mean, and what is it?

A hermaphrodite is an individual that is androgynous. The word hermaphrodite comes from the Greek gods Hermes (who was male) and Aphrodite (who was female). You could say that hermaphrodite is the biological term for androgyny.

Some animals are simultaneous hermaphrodites. That is, they have two sexes simultaneously. These include earthworms, leeches, sponges, slugs, and snails, but also other groups of animals, such as corals, flatworms, polychaete worms, crustaceans, bryozoans, sea squirts, and fish.

Shrimp, however, have one sex at a time, but are also included among hermaphrodites. They are born as males, but will become females after the first reproductive cycle.

Earthworms are hermaphrodites and produce both eggs and sperm, but they cannot self-fertilize without exchanging sperm with each other first. At the "pairing," the two worms settle with their front ends overlapping. They then secrete a mucus, which encases them. Sperm is emitted into the mucus and is passed, through muscle movements, to the opening of the partner's body, where they are joined. After the worms exchange sperm in this way, they separate. Later, the worm secretes a mucus sleeve around itself. The worm crawls backwards, out of this sleeve, and injects its own eggs and the sperm from the other worm into it. When the worm crawls completely out of the mucus sleeve, the process is over. Fertilization occurs in the sleeve and new worms are created.

Medicinal leeches—like all other leeches—are hermaphroditic and lay eggs in cocoons that also contain nutrient stores, which are saved for future use. The cocoon is secreted by a thickening of the body, a so-called girdle (clitellum), where the male and female sex organs exist. For fertilization, one specimen acts as sperm donor and the other as sperm recipient. Cocoons, with up to 15 eggs in each, are deposited in moist ground near the shore in July. After a few months baby leeches creep out and make their way to the water.

Slugs are hermaphrodites. Slug reproduction most often occurs by mating and exchanging sperm, but self-fertilization also occurs. Thus it can be enough for a single slug or a single egg to arrive at a new location for an entirely new population to emerge. One example of this is the dreaded killer slug.

A slug can reproduce in several ways, depending on the variety. Most marine slugs are single gendered—meaning that they have either testes or ovaries—while the terrestrial and freshwater slugs are hermaphrodites.

5
QUICKIES

Are animals sexually attracted to individuals of the same sex?

Yes, it occurs. For example, it happens with the males of some bird species that grow up together, isolated from the company of others.

How do courtship and sexual intercourse differ between same-sex and other-sex pairs?

They are similar. Animal courtship and mating behaviors are often ritualized and fixed. The animals do not have great ability to alter or vary these.

What are the benefits of sex beyond procreation?

For one thing, it strengthens the unity between two individuals or groups of individuals.

Does the energy lost during intercourse correspond to the benefits it brings?

Hardly. But animals do not think or consider the way we humans do; their behavior is more innate. (Even human beings often don't think when it comes to this particular topic!) It is possible that some "thinking" may affect the great apes (Hominidae).

Are animals aware that same-sex intercourse and masturbation do not lead to offspring?

No. But this is a difficult question. "Consciousness" (of their own existence or consequences of behavior) hardly exists in animals. Again, it is possible that the great apes have a degree of consciousness. Maybe not. It is difficult to determine.

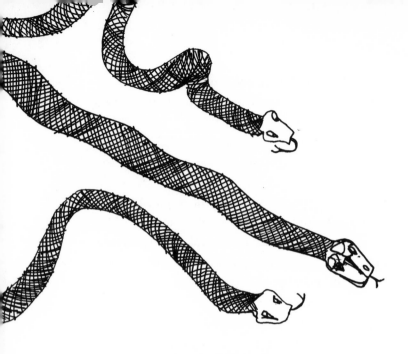

How do snakes mate?

Late April is mating season for many snakes. At that time, snakes gather in abundance. Each female usually has a whole group of males following her. Mating takes place in just one day, and then all the snakes disperse.

The eggs, which often stick together, are laid in June or July, or sometimes even August. A female snake can lay 5–50 eggs, depending on her size; however, there are usually only 5–15 eggs. After that, she cares for neither the eggs nor the babies when they are hatched. Eggs are laid in a warm place, often in a type of compost or in a dunghill where thermal decomposition helps the eggs develop faster. In the beginning, babies subsist on bugs, but when they get older they start to eat fish, frogs, toads, and other smaller animals.

They say the Apollo butterfly has a chastity belt. Is it true?

Yes, that's right. After mating, the male pastes waxy balls in and around the female's abdomen (called a sphragis). This includes both additional semen and other important nutrients that increase the chances of a successful conception. A sphragis also functions as a kind of protection—which can be likened to a chastity belt—that prevents the female from mating with additional males.

What determines whether a "bird marriage" lasts for life depends, in principle, only on nesting success and death. If the desired number of children is not reached, birds simply get new partners. So, too, if a partner dies.

So it is a myth that all swans mate for life.

THE BIGGEST!

The Argentine ruddy duck, *Oxyura vittata*, is a giant in terms of penis size (14–16 inches). Among the limited species of birds in the world that have a penis, there appear to be very few species that can compare with *O. vittata*. Its penis can actually be a full 17 inches long!

All six *Oxyura* species have a similar routine in which the penis is exhibited when the males compete for females in groups.

AMERICAN COMPETITION

The evidence suggests that it is the length of the penis that makes the American ruddy duck, *Oxyura jamaicensis*, a threat to ruddy duck *O. leucocephala*, whose females clearly prefer the American kin that have been introduced to their native habitat in recent years.

Is the lion lazy? Yes and no.

Many who have seen lions in a zoo or in the wild believe that they, especially the males, are lazy animals. They seem mostly to lie down and rest, or lumber around leisurely. This accusation is both true and false. Lions usually sleep a full twenty hours a day and are wise enough not to waste energy unnecessarily. But it is also true that lions can mate, or copulate, up to 60–80 times per day, all during the approximately four hours that they are awake. And this is necessary, as it has been calculated that an average of 3,000 copulations are performed for each cub that reaches adulthood. So they are not just idle.

LION FACTS

Lions are the only species of the cat family that live socially.

The lion is the only species of the cat family in which males and females have different appearances.

The male lion is the only male in the cat family that has a mane.

The lion can attack at a speed of 35–50 miles per hour. At leisure, it travels 2.5 miles per hour.

Can all cats climb trees?

No, cheetahs, unlike other cats, cannot climb trees. Particularly good at climbing is the margay (found in South America), which spends almost all of its life in the trees. The clouded leopard is also a great climber and has a long tail (the longest of all cat species), which it uses to maintain balance while running in the trees.

SABERTOOTH

The clouded leopard, which lives in the Southeast Asia, is also the feline with the longest canine teeth relative to body size. Clouded leopard teeth, unlike those of other cat species, evolved from the saber-toothed cat *Smilodon*, which lived tens of thousands of years ago.

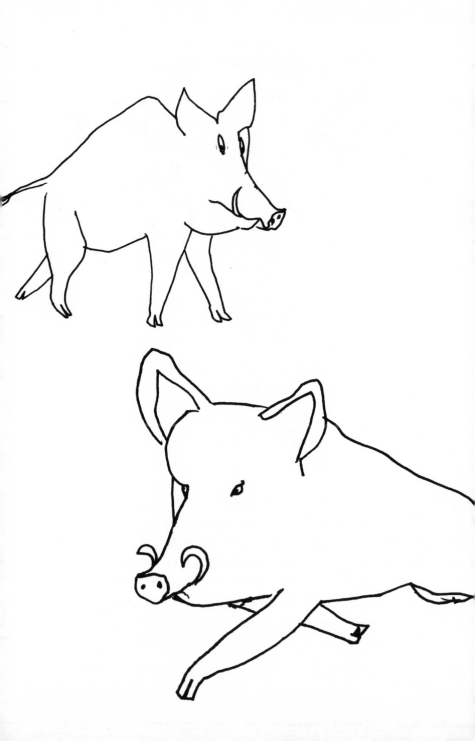

A QUESTION OF STATUS

How does a herd of boars rank?

Wild pigs are social animals and, for much of the year, they live in groups containing sows with piglets. When the babies reach the age of one year and the new piglets are to be born, they are expelled from the group to start their own communities. The sows can later rejoin the original group—with or without their own piglets—and thus form even larger herds of up to 50 individuals.

The herd is led by the oldest female—the head sow. In large flocks, she is the head of all subgroups (in rare cases, however, others, particularly powerful sows, dominate subgroups). The head sow leads hikes, decides where foraging occurs, protects the offspring, and suckles newborns.

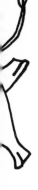

Young expelled boars sometimes form small groups from the same litter. They have created a hierarchy among themselves already as piglets. This type of group is short-lived and dissolves when boars reach about the age of two.

Boars older than two years live as loners, except during mating season. When they choose, usually between October and January, they join the roving wild boar groups.

The wild pig has a long history in Sweden, going back more than 8,000 years. The wild pig was hunted for several reasons and exterminated in the late 1600s.

While domestic pigs were allowed to go loose in the woods and there were wild pigs in the area, they mixed freely with each other. This was one of the reasons why they became extinct. In the mid-1970s fenced wild boar were contained in the area of Trosa, Björkvik, and the Kila Valley in Södermanland. They managed to establish themselves there, and wild pigs have since increased in numbers and spread. In the 2000s, wild pigs were observed in all counties in southern Sweden. Their continued spread northward will likely go more slowly. Although they tolerate cold, the snow impedes their progress during the winter and makes food inaccessible, while also making them easier prey for wolves and other predators.

For a long time, man has been the wild pig's foremost enemy. We have hunted them for thousands of years. Natural threats to wild pigs are wolves and bears, which are the only predators that can take down adult boars. Fox and lynx can take piglets.

Recently, wild boars have started to become a problem for traffic in Sweden.

The uprooting of the forest environment caused by wild pigs has been described as both positive and negative. The positive is that it facilitates forest regeneration. A great diversity of plants has been noted growing in the soil, according to some surveys. Particularly beneficial is the distribution of seeds and moss propagules. But rooting can also have negative effects, by destroying the roots and disseminating spruce root rot.

Additionally, rooting is bad for farmland. On mowing embankments harvested for silage, the soil bacteria will destroy the harvest and ensiling. Damage to agricultural crops also occurs when the pigs go out into the fields and trample the harvest to access mature grains like corn, and to eat crops like peas and potatoes. The greatest damage is probably done on small areas of agricultural land that are protected by forest.

Similarly, among the wolves, the female wolf is the most powerful. A wolf pack usually consists of a pair of leaders—the alpha couple—and their offspring from one or more years. This is a strategy that has proven to work well for millennia: The survival of individuals has increased, which has allowed this strategy to continue. Herds improve the hunt and provide education to the next generation of pups.

In the pack there is a clear hierarchy with the alpha female at the top. The alpha female controls the alpha male and other females. The alpha male dominates only the other males. Communication within the pack is extremely important and the structure is complex and complicated. Wolves communicate with each other by smell, movement patterns, and facial expressions. Wolves become sexually mature at two or three years and then the young often leave, especially males, to flock together with a new female and create a new pack. In principle, only the alpha couple may have cubs in a pack. The older siblings often act as babysitters.

The fox often returns to the hen house to kill several chickens despite being full. Why?

When a fox (or a wolf, in a sheep pasture) sees a live animal, this acts as a fundamental stimulus and the animal's hunting behavior is triggered, even if it is already full. Under natural conditions, this situation would never arise because the rest of the herd would run away, but in a chicken farm or a pasture, the animals have nowhere to go. It is important to understand that it is not "bloodlust" or that predators find it "fun" to kill prey. This is an innate behavior that is controlled by the animal's genes, and the animal cannot control the behavior consciously.

THE OWL STAYS IN PLACE

Compare this to the Eurasian pygmy owl, which accumulates stores of food for the cold winter, when it is normally short of food. It captures a great deal of prey (mice, voles, small birds) and stashes it high up, such as in an old woodpecker's nest. But this is a behavior that has a specific function—it is an adaptation to withstand harsh conditions. Again, it is not a question of bloodlust.

How do crocodiles hunt?

Crocodiles are carnivores. They usually eat about every two weeks, but can survive without food for up to two years because they are cold-blooded (i.e., ectothermic) and can save their energy. They usually catch their prey in the water by sneaking up on it almost silently. When they get hold of prey, they drag it down under the water and hold it there until it drowns.

But crocodiles can actually jump out of the water several feet for something new to eat—for example, a bird flying in the air or a land animal that sits in a tree.

The crocodile's jaws and digestive system are designed so that the crocodile can eat everything from insects, fish, and birds to large mammals such as wildebeests and antelopes, and it can even swallow prey whole.

Like mammals, their teeth are in a jaw bone, but crocodile teeth are replaced continuously throughout a lifetime. Each tooth is hollow, and a new tooth is always growing inside an existing tooth. A crocodile can produce up to 3,000 teeth in a long life.

Almost nothing is known about how old crocodiles can be in the wild, but most likely they can live to be about 100 years old.

According to a popular myth that was established by Herodotus in the 5th century BC, the African crocodile would use a bird sometimes called a crocodile bird as a toothbrush. The crocodile, according to this myth, would let the bird eat meat scraps stuck between its teeth.

SINGLE IS STRONG—OR GROUP WORK

Group-hunting predators, like lions and hyenas, are able to take larger prey than solitary hunting predators. In some circumstances, the benefit of group hunting is likely that the social way of life can be maintained and strengthened. It is evident that sociality in these species is a highly complex phenomenon, and there is currently no unequivocal answer to why some species live socially and others do not. All predator species differ in their hunting methods. These differences may possibly be related to the social organization of both hunter and prey, and partly explain why different predators can live side by side.

Cheetahs hunt by stealth and tremendous speed, up to over 60 miles per hour, and overrunning their prey. The prey is not killed merely by being knocked over. The cheetah must use its large, sharp, and dramatically curved claw, which is located a bit up on the inner leg. If they are not able to succeed within a few hundred yards they give up, probably because their bodies cannot handle any greater increase in temperature. Such high-speed pursuits require a reasonably clear view with a lack of obstructing bushes and trees. Generally, cheetahs only hunt in broad daylight. Cheetahs are the only predators that eat only what they have killed themselves. Another of their peculiarities is that they cannot retract their claws the way other cats can.

Hyenas hunt in groups and in the open countryside. They can pursue an animal up to nearly 2 miles before plunging over the exhausted prey. Trees, shrubs, and other natural obstacles are more of a minor inconvenience for the pursuer than the pursued, but may nonetheless cause a disadvantage because it can make it difficult to keep track of the fleeing prey. Typically, hyenas chase at night, when their night vision gives them an advantage over prey.

Leopards hunt alone, mostly at night, by slowly sneaking up on prey, surprising it altogether, or sprinting for short distances. Such a method of hunting requires considerable assistance from trees, shrubs, and grasses. The vegetation in the Serengeti woodlands offers this assistance, and you will not find any leopards in savannahs.

Lions use essentially the same hunting technique as leopards, with the difference being that lions hunt in groups. A number of lions spread out around a defined area and sneak up on the prey. When the prey becomes aware of a lion rushing, it will run in the opposite direction, and will hopefully—from the lion's perspective—run within reach of the other lions. Group hunting helps the lion to hunt successfully in a habitat with less natural camouflage than would otherwise be required. Lions also primarily hunt at night.

Did you know that...

... the spotted hyena has the strongest bite of any land predator and can crush the largest bones of a prey or carcass?

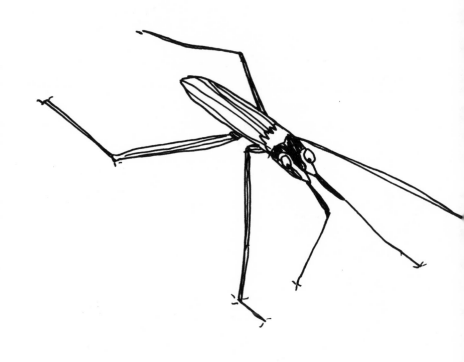

HOW IS THAT POSSIBLE?

How can water bugs walk on water?

Water bugs cannot swim, so they're lucky that they can walk on water instead. Since the water bug rests both its feet and its lower legs on the water surface, the surface area the bug spreads over the water is great. This allows it to make good use of water resistance. The water bug may appear to have only four legs but, like all other insects, it has six legs, though the two front legs are small and serve as claws for catching prey. The rear legs act as rudders, so only the middle legs are used to run on water.

The water bug runs around on the water to find other bugs that have fallen in and are struggling. Water bugs are chiefly predators and, just like their relatives, the backswimmers and water boatmen, they have a proboscis that they stick in the fallen prey.

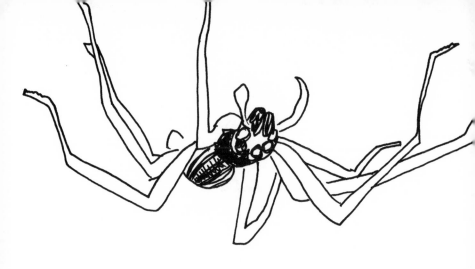

How can spiders walk on the ceiling without falling off?

A spider has claws on its feet that are used for gripping. These can be seen with a magnifying glass. But a spider also has very small hairs on its feet that can only be seen with a very strong microscope. One spider foot contains 78,000 of these hairs. These little hairs allow the spider to get a foothold in the ceiling by increasing friction against the surface—the more hair the better. Provided all eight legs are on the ceiling at the same time, there are total of 624,000 hairs supporting a spider that weighs generally .0005 ounces. This provides security for the spider 160 times over; that is, the force holding the spider to the ceiling is capable, in principle, of supporting a spider 160 times heavier!

Do ants move?

Most ants will remain in the same hill for a lifetime, but in the summer new queens and males hatch. Both queens and males have wings. As if on cue, all these newly hatched individuals leave the hill at the same time, and so do other ants from other hills nearby. When they land, males look for a queen to mate with. After mating, the males die. The fertilized queen bites off her flight wings, or the worker ants do this for her. The queen then forms a new hill, alone or with the help of some workers. But the queen can also be transferred back to the old hill or to an existing hill nearby.

How do you get rid of an anthill?

Many people have a variety of reasons to get rid of nearby anthills.

Ideally, of course, you should allow the anthill to remain. But if the ants chose to create their nest in a completely hopeless location, there is a method that usually works: Insert an iron rod in the anthill in the fall and leave it in place through the winter. In the spring, you will discover that the ants have moved out. The iron rod cools down the interior of the anthill, and this is not appreciated by the ants, with their intricate network of passageways and chambers. As it is not easy to take on an object as large as an iron rod, it is easier to move to a new hill.

Ants are excellent at spreading plant seeds, so if you want a flowery garden, you should keep them. Many plants have a fatty outgrowth called an elaiosome (an outgrowth of the oil-rich cells of the fruit or seeds of some plants). The ant takes the elaiosome to its hill and uses it as food for the larvae. Many times, however, the ant eats the fat on its way to the hill, and when the fat is eaten, the ant discards the undamaged seed because it no longer serves as a food source. Seed dispersal by ants is called myrmecochory.

5
QUICKIES

How old can an ant get?
A worker ant can live to be a few weeks old, while a queen may live to be at least a year old.

How much can an ant carry?
An ant can carry seven times its own weight, which is .0004 ounces. It can drag small things, like dry plant matter, dead insects, and berries (at most .0028 ounces), to the hill. Together, several ants can manage even greater burdens, such as a dead hornet (weighing approximately .007 ounces).

How does an ant move?
An ant has six legs with three on each side of the body. A walking ant uses its legs such that the first (the front) and third (the rear) on one side move forward with the second (the middle) leg on the opposite side. This means that the two hind legs are never used simultaneously, and this is true of all insects.

How long can an ant run?
An ant never runs, but it can go fast.

How small are ants when they are born?
An ant has an exoskeleton and becomes neither larger nor smaller after birth.

Are they surviving or moving?

It is well known that a lot of worms tend to show up after heavy or prolonged rain. The usual explanation for this is that the worms would drown when their tunnels would flood. Worms breathe through their skin by taking in oxygen from the air that normally fills the tunnels, and if the aisles were flooded, the worms might not get enough oxygen.

But could it be that this is not just a matter of survival, but also of relocating? The reason would be that the worms would not run the risk of becoming dehydrated when leaving the safe, damp earth. This explanation could very well be true, but on one condition: the move is done at night, or at least under very overcast conditions. Worms cannot withstand ultraviolet light. Exposed to UV radiation, worms die relatively quickly and therefore, they are never found above ground in sunshine unless forced. A rainy day would be an ideal time to move to a new home.

How can a bird sleep standing on one foot?

A safe and secure sleeping bird is usually perched on one leg with the second tucked up under the body. Birds have a locking mechanism that helps them hold position, but also to maintain themselves on branches. Many sleeping birds twist their heads toward their backs and place their bills in their back feathers, while others place their beaks among their breast feathers.

Some birds rest on one leg, while others draw their legs up into their feathers, especially in cold weather. Many ground-dwelling birds, like quail and pheasant, sleep in trees. A few parrots (of the genus *Loriculus*) sleep hanging upside down. Some hummingbirds fall into torpor at night, and their metabolic rates drop sharply.

✦ MYTH ✦

If we are to believe the record books, the peregrine falcon can reach a diving speed of over 220 miles per hour. The origin of this figure is uncertain, but it has been around at least since the middle of last century. Nature filmmaker Jan Lindblad made a film in the 1960s in which he filmed a diving peregrine falcon. Using film camera speed he was able to figure out that the peregrines moved at a speed of around 100 miles per hour. Legitimate data today indicates that a peregrine falcon can dive at speeds of around, or even a little over, 125 miles per hour when crash diving for prey.

Did you know that...

. . . a diving gannet can enter the water at a speed of 90 miles per hour?

Can animals cry?

Tears do not always mean that you are sad; they serve to keep the eyes' mucous membranes moist and elastic, and allow the friction between the eye and eyelid to decrease when blinking.

The only animal that can cry is man; there are no other animals that can cry, as we do, with tears dropping. However, there are certainly many animal species that feel sorrow, but their emotion manifests itself in ways other than crying and tears.

In male elephants, a runny liquid that is reminiscent of tears comes from the temporal glands that sit alongside the eyes. This occurs during periods of increased testosterone (a sex hormone) production, known as musth (or must), and these periods usually last between 2 weeks and 5 months.

Superficial damage to the cornea of a cat or dog heals normally within a few days. But until then, it hurts. The cat or dog squints or pinches the eye. The tears then flow and the cat or dog is careful with the eye. Most likely, it may also be that the tears in the eyes of cats and dogs serve to moisten the cornea.

To get rid of excess salt, many reptiles and birds have developed special salt glands through which they can secrete a highly concentrated salt solution. The actual discharge of brine can be made via the nasal cavity (in birds and lizards), the mouth (in sea snakes and crocodiles), or through the eye sockets (in turtles). In sea turtles, these may look like tears, but these are not due to sadness, but due to elevated salt concentration in the body.

What can jump the highest?

One candidate is the spectral tarsier, *Tarsier spectrum*, which has a height of 3–6 inches. These little animals are great jumpers: They can jump up to 10 times their own body height, 5 feet straight up and 6–10 feet horizontally. From tree to tree, they can jump up to 20 feet high.

The ability to jump high offers several advantages to animals, including access to places that are hard to reach, and escape from predators.

Javier Sotomayor's world record of 2.45 meters (just over 8 feet) is about one and a half times his own body height. But in general, froghoppers—the insects behind frothy foam on plants in nature, for which the cuckoo was once blamed—can jump over 100 times their own body height—from a standstill! A 0.2-inch-long frog-hopper can jump as high as 27.5 inches. The flea can jump over 200 times its own body height, but relative to body weight, it is the froghopper that accomplishes the greater feat.

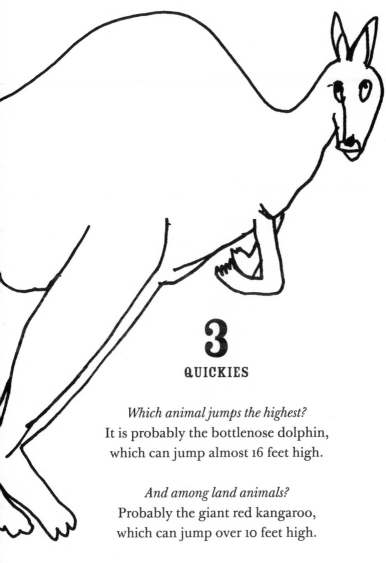

3

QUICKIES

Which animal jumps the highest?
It is probably the bottlenose dolphin,
which can jump almost 16 feet high.

And among land animals?
Probably the giant red kangaroo,
which can jump over 10 feet high.

Anything else?
Of note is the white-tailed deer, which
can jump just over 8 feet high.

How far can a/an _____ jump?

edible snail	0.0 feet
flea	1.3 feet
weasel	3.0 feet
ermine	5.6 feet
cat	7.5 feet
hare	9.2 feet
squirrel	10–13 feet
red deer	12.1 feet
katydid	14.8 feet
deer	22.2 feet
moose	13.1 feet (in some cases possibly up to 32.8 feet)
lynx	32.8 feet
frog	33.8 feet
puma	36.1 feet
hare	39.4 feet (on a slight downhill incline)
red kangaroo	42 feet

Did you know that . . .

. . . a snow leopard has been seen jumping over an approximately 50-foot ditch? Compare that to Mike Powell's world record jump in 1991 when he jumped 8.95 meters (29.4 feet).

A BIT ABOUT
HOW IT WORKS

LIFE

What is life?

We all have a fairly good idea of what "life" means. However, there is, to my knowledge, no generally accepted definition. If one were to attempt to make a definition of the word "life," it should include such things as:

→ metabolism
→ energy metabolism
→ ability to reproduce
→ ability to perceive environmental conditions
→ ability to maintain a fluid, thermodynamic state of imbalance
→ development (i.e., evolution)

Which came first, the chicken or the egg?

The chicken is a bird, and birds are descended from other egg-laying mammals. So the egg definitely came before the chicken.

What is an animal?

What is the minimum requirement for something to be considered an animal? What about coral? And what is different about a plant or a fungus?

Let's start with the minimum: an organism is a biological entity capable of replication or of transferring genetic material. The definition of organism includes, besides plants, animals, etc., even such things as seeds and pollen.

Plants and animals are composed of cells with a true nucleus surrounded by a thin film, a membrane (which is why they are called eukaryotic, meaning "with a true nucleus").

Animals are multicellular organisms that are part of the animal kingdom. They are mobile and depend on eating other living or dead organisms for their survival. With few exceptions, animals have muscles, a nervous system, and an internal cavity in the body, intended for the digestion of food.

Unlike plants, animal body cells are not enclosed in a shell of cellulose, and they cannot utilize carbohydrates by photosynthesis the way plants do, but are instead dependent on the consumption of other organisms to acquire this energy content.

What is a species?

There are a number of ways to define what a species is. The most common and easiest, but not the most comprehensive, is a definition that goes something like this:

A species is a group of individuals that can reproduce with each other under natural conditions, and that are reproductively isolated from other groups of individuals. Individuals of the same species can thus, at least potentially, and if they belong to different sexes, have joint sex capable of producing offspring.

But this definition, which is called the biological species concept, is not particularly useful for organisms in which the offspring are produced asexually (budding, vegetative propagation, parthenogenesis/virgin birth, division, sprouting) or by self-fertilization.

Besides the biological species concept, there are alternative species concepts, such as the "evolutionary," which is based on mate choice, and the "organic," which focuses on togetherness. And then there are two types of so-called phylogenetic species concepts.

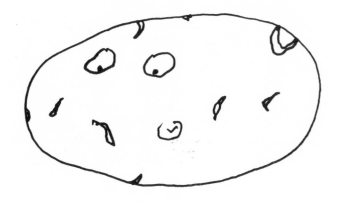

Why can't potatoes walk?

To get food, animals move. They can walk, run, crawl, curl, swim, fly, or otherwise make their way to get food. A plant, however, receives its food from the soil and the ground through its root system, and therefore does not move.

The potato—a perennial that grows approximately 20 inches high—cannot walk, but it can move, albeit very slowly, perhaps only an inch or so a year. Potatoes reproduce vegetatively, by cloning, so that the new, underground, and nutrient-storing tubers (potatoes) come up a short distance higher than the previous year. So it can go, year after year, and after 100 years the plant may move a few feet. Because of the fact that it's the same genetic material in the corms that returns year after year, one could say that the potato is a plant that can be thousands of years old, perhaps one of the oldest plants we have.

PERUVIAN NIGHTSHADE AND EARTH-PEARS

The potato, *Solanum tuberosum*, originated in South America, where it was first cultivated 10,000 years ago. The Spaniard de Quesada brought the potato to Europe (Spain) for the first time in 1539. How the potato arrived in Sweden is partly shrouded in mystery. It was likely Olof Rudbeck who brought the first potato to Sweden, and this would have occurred around 1655. Rudbeck called his new delicacy Peruvian Nightshade. Not until the 1720s did Jonas Alströmer bring the potato to France. He called them earth-pears, a term that still exists in Skåne.

KNOWN RELATIVES

In the family Solanaceae, there are 90 genera and 2,600 species throughout the world. In Sweden there are about a dozen genera and nearly 20 species, and most of them are occasional weeds or cultivated species that have been naturalized, such as the tomato. Another well-known genus is tobacco, *Nicotiana*, of which two species were formerly grown in Sweden for the manufacturing of tobacco products. The family also includes several herbs often associated with witches and witchcraft, such as henbane, *Hyoscyamus niger*, jimsonweed, *Datura stramonium*, deadly nightshade, *Atropa belladonna*, and the legendary mandrake, *Mandragora officinarum*.

105

Potatoes can be attacked by a large number of vermin—rodents, nematodes, mollusks, centipedes, insects, spiders, and crustaceans—but they can also be eaten by larger animals like cranes and wild boar.

Cranes can cause damage to newly planted potato fields through their search for potato plants. It is not the newly planted potato plant they seek, but the 6-month-old or older potatoes. Cranes do whatever is necessary to find newly sprouted potatoes and have little or no interest at all in the potato waste they leave on the ground.

Pigs are happy to snatch up the potatoes that are left after the harvest, but not until there has been frost on the ground, when the potatoes become a bit softer. At freezing temperatures, the starch is turned to sugar in potatoes, which the pigs eagerly await.

Did you know that...

... when potatoes are exposed to light, chlorophyll is produced and can turn them green? Other toxic and bitter tasting substances, such as solanine, which occurs naturally in all potato plants, are also produced as protection against attack by fungi and bacteria. Solanine is toxic and in large doses can even be fatal to both animals and humans.

❖ MYTH ❖

"If you split a worm in half, it grows into two worms." Hmm. Yes and no.

Worm is a common name for a large number of animals. So, worms can be easily confused with other animals. For example, the "worm" in an apple is really a caterpillar. There are even snakes and amphibians—vertebrates—that look like worms, but are not. Well, now to the point: Will an earthworm split in half develop into two complete individuals? (Entirely beside the point, of course, is that this is not their normal mode of reproduction.)

Yes and no. In Sweden there are about 40 earthworm species (of the family Lumbricidae). They can regenerate lost body segments, and it is the front that can survive and develop a new tail, but it depends a bit on where the worm is severed.

However, there is actually an aquatic worm (which also belongs to the family Lumbriculidae) of which both parts can survive and become new worms.

Natural selection—what is it?

Selection indicates choice and, in an evolutionary context, it means that some organisms have more young that survive to adulthood than others. In nature, it works such that individuals with certain special properties that increase the chance of survival have more offspring in their lifetimes than individuals with other characteristics. These offspring will also benefit by having more offspring, and so on. This type of selection is called natural selection.

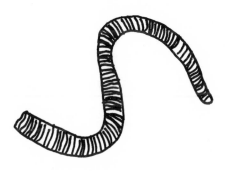

MECHANISMS AND RAW MATERIALS

Natural selection is the mechanism behind evolution. The raw material for evolution, however, is the genetic variation, (i.e., the fact that the genome varies as much as it does). Natural selection maintains genetic variation because habitats vary and different characteristics evolve in different environments to adapt to them. Those who are strongest and smartest, or the most adaptable, survive.

Which animal is the oldest?

If we limit this to mammals, man is probably the mammal that can live the longest, with a maximum life span of 110–120 years. The great apes do not get as old: the chimpanzee is said to live to 40–50 years old, and the gorilla for more than 50 years. As a general rule for mammals, the bigger they are, the older they get. Man is not typical, because he gets very old despite his relatively low body weight. The Indian elephant tends to live 70–80 years in the wild, and the African elephant lives 50–60 years. There is not much information on the large whale species. I've seen estimates that large whales can live to be up to 100 years old, and even 130. If this is true, several whale species compete with humans for being the oldest mammal.

Seemingly credible information indicates that harpoon blades of stone and ivory were recently found in bowhead whales. The Inuit stopped using such harpoons in the mid-1800s. These whales would therefore have been considerably more than 100 years old. The harpoon findings prompted researchers to try to determine the age of bowhead whales using the age-related changes in the proteins that make up the eye lens. Most of the proteins in the body regenerate continuously, with the old ones broken down and new ones constantly forming. An exception is the protein in the eye lens. The protein in the back of the lens is thus original to the moment when the lens was constructed in the fetus. Age-related changes in the human lens can lead to eye disease (cataract), in which the lens becomes cloudy

110

and vision gradually deteriorates. When the lenses of a number of bowhead whales killed between 1978 and 1996 were examined, they found that 5 whales must have been more than 100 years old when they died. One of these whales was determined to be 211 years old! The whale may be the oldest known mammal.

"LONESOME GEORGE"

Looking at vertebrates as a whole, there are giant tortoises that can be 150–200 years old. The most famous of all turtles, "Lonesome George" of the Galapagos Islands, was estimated to be only 70–80 years old. He wore his gloomy name because he was the last of his subspecies before he died in 2012.

The giant tortoise and the bowhead whale are perhaps the ones that are the oldest. A frontrunner is a tortoise in India that was brought from the Seychelles 130 years ago, and it was 255 years old when it died in captivity. There are also mussels that compete for the title.

Moreover, there may, of course, be other elderly that have not yet been discovered!

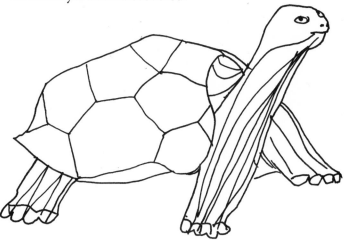

WOLF TRACKS, THEN AND NOW

How did the wolf become the wolf?

During the Paleocene epoch (about 60 million years ago), there was a specialized raccoon-like carnivore called *Miacis*. From this, canines, bears, badgers, and weasels developed. Canines evolved on the North American continent about 30 million years ago. Then, 10 to 20 million years later (during the Miocene epoch), a small canine with a narrow skull appeared, and that is believed to be the ancestor of the coyote.

The first wolf species arose between 4.7 and 1.8 million years ago. Among the first known species are *Canis priscolatrans*, a small, wolf-like red fox that colonized Europe and Asia by crossing the land bridge Beringia, now the Bering Strait.

From *C. priscolatrans* evolved *Canis etruscus* and then *Canis mosbachensis*. The primitive wolves—which look very similar to the modern southern populations of wolves found in the Arabian Peninsula and South Asia—spread across Europe in the early Pleistocene ice age, about 500,000 years ago. *C. mosbachensis* evolved into *Canis lupus*, and recolonized North America during the geological period known as Rancholabrean (300,000 to 11,000 BC). At that time the dire wolf, *Canis dirus,* was already in North America. But the large prey that the dire wolf chiefly lived off of died out, and the competition with the newly introduced wolves that had smaller prey may have contributed to the extinction of the dire wolf 8,000 years ago. With the dire wolf's disappearance, the modern wolf became the only remaining large and widespread canine animal.

Did you know that...

...today's dogs descended from wolves? The species diverged about 100,000 years ago.

How dangerous is a wolf?

In principle, it is a fact that all animals can be dangerous to humans. Wolves and other animals typically shy away from people, but if the animals are backed into a corner, they will obviously try to get away; then come their defense and escape instincts. Since we seriously began researching wolves in the 1960s, very few deaths caused by wolves have been documented in the Western world. In 2006, a 22-year-old student was killed by wolves during a walk in northern Saskatchewan, Canada. Through the tracks in the snow, the whole process could be followed. The 22-year-old tried to escape and was knocked to the ground. He had managed to get up and ran a bit further before the wolves finally killed him. In 1963, a 5-year-old boy was killed in Quebec, Canada. In Sweden, there have been no known deaths caused by wolves.

The wolf's most common prey are ungulates—such as the moose and the deer—but they also eat fish, birds, insects, reptiles, and amphibians. During the summer they frequently eat small rodents, hares, and beavers. The wolf can also trap deer, foxes, and sheep. During the winter, wolves hunt in packs and take down moose, reindeer, and farm animals.

THE MODERN WOLF

How should we behave toward the modern wolf? There are many opinions, and today the resistance against wolves in Sweden comes from many sources, not primarily by the authorities, as it did in the 1700s. Perhaps we can learn a thing or two about how we could live side by side with the wolf, as they do in Italy, where there may be 500 wolves living in densely populated areas of 60 million people, yet encounters between humans and wolves are very rare. Wolves are in close proximity to sheep farmers. An effective fence is pretty safe, but not as good as shepherds and dogs. With shepherds and guard dogs in cooperation, the sheep can be protected at a rate of nearly 100 percent if they are also brought into barns at night. Up to 300 sheep need only one shepherd and two guard dogs. Sheep owners in Italy have learned that the combination works great against predators. Wolves do get one from time to time, but that is very little in comparison with the 5–10 percent of the animals that die a natural death. Could the same be done in Sweden or elsewhere as they have done in Italy?

116

How do you know how many there are?

When determining the populations of the big four of Sweden (wolves, bears, lynx, and wolverines) it is best to try to do it when there is snow. At that time, it is easier to follow the trails, especially with wolves and lynx. Wolf litters can also be noted on the bare ground through surveys of dens or meeting places used by wolves during the summer, for example.

A wolverine census should be conducted mainly during the late winter through locating wolverine dens and observing the number of offspring. Bears can be counted in a number of different ways, such as by observation of females with cubs reported by the public and hunters. Additionally, an inventory was made based on DNA from bear droppings a few years ago.

THE ART OF TRACKING

When it comes to tracking, it is usually a professional tracker who is out in the field, looking for tracks where it is believed that the animals are. Note that the quality of track characteristics is rarely as clear in reality as it is in images, and can therefore be difficult to interpret. Even tracks from the same individual may exhibit large variations in appearance depending on whether they are from front or back paws, which gait the animal used, how fast the animal moved, how deeply the paw was pressed into snow, and so on. Footprints may also vary depending on the ground; if it is hard, a shallow imprint is made, and if it is soft, a deeper imprint will be made.

Trackers follow every footprint and seek to answer the following questions: Which species made the track or tracks, how many individuals were there, have they all gone in the same direction, have they all gone together, are there territorial markings of any sort that can indicate the animal's social status, and are there any other observations that should be documented?

GETTING TO THE SOURCE

When you find a track, more often than not you should follow it backwards, not forwards. That way, you can then see what possible prey the animal encountered, and if you're lucky you can find droppings or tufts of hair. With knowledge of how animals behave, you can determine what species left the droppings, and what prey it ate. And with the help of DNA tests from droppings and hair tufts, it is even easier to determine the species.

THE POACHER WAS HELPED

You can also capture individuals and put radio transmitters on them. These use a GPS transmitter that sends data containing coordinates from the ground (via small antennae), which is then obtained by the GSM network and loaded directly into a computer. The data from older models of transmitters were able to be intercepted by unauthorized persons, like poachers, which sadly meant that those who were determined to protect an animal sometimes led the poacher right to it. This is no longer a risk with the newest technology.

ON THE SAVANNAH

Why do animals on the savannah migrate?

One of nature's most spectacular and famous sights is the migration (trekking) of herbivores that move in the Serengeti and Masai Mara in East Africa. We've seen it in film and television since the 1960s, but it is equally fascinating each time. Mainly, these are wildebeests (specifically, white-bearded wildebeests) and in that area have a population of approximately 1.5 million individuals. A similar migration pattern is also exhibited by zebras and Thomson's gazelles.

From November to January, depending on when the "short" rains begin, the main migration eastward begins. And in May, at the end of the "long" rains, they migrate back. In fact, the movement is continuous through the year (so-called mini-migrations), but on these two occasions there is conspicuous movement of most of the animals, almost simultaneously. The definitive start of the great shake-up comes quickly, and may be caused by a sudden change in weather, such as a heavy rainstorm. When the bulk of the wildebeests start their trek westward in May, they move from the savannah's short grass to the bushland of the north and west, where there is permanent water. There they remain for the next 5 months until the "short" rains begin again. Then they begin to retreat to the grassy savannahs, and thus complete a year's hiking cycle.

GRASS AND RAIN CONTROL

The main reason that some animals migrate from one place to another seems to be related to food supply. Wildebeests and zebras eat almost exclusively grass, but of different quality. Thomson's gazelles, on the other hand, gladly eat things other than grass: dicotyledonous plants, particularly protein-rich fruits. Zebras tolerate grasses of the worst and coarsest quality, and are therefore the first of the three species to occupy an area of tall grass. Wildebeests will follow in succession and fill themselves with the better parts of the grass that zebras leave behind. Finally come the small Thomson's gazelles, which require high-quality food. Where the wildebeests have grazed, fresh grass has come up again, and other herbs, which were previously difficult to reach among the long grasses, are exposed for the gazelles.

Migrations are thus determined by food availability, which in turn is dependent upon rain. Annual variations in migration patterns are related to rainfall. The animals only graze on savannahs if they can produce enough grass. During dry periods, the wildebeests utilize the wetter forests and richer areas. This flexibility is essential in an environment where rainfall is very unpredictable.

EATING IN FLOCKS

Joining a group and eating together has often been interpreted as a protective measure against predators, but this behavior is also considered to have significant energy implications for grazing animals. Of course, the height of the grass diminishes, but relatively recent studies show that the concentration of the biomass increases to more than double in a cooperatively grazed field compared to an uncooperatively grazed one.

Intensive grazing causes the grass to grow out again quickly; hence, new and energy-rich shoots come up all the time. A grass-fed individual in a herd has greater opportunities to obtain energy-rich grass of high quality, which increases the efficiency of food intake.

Why are animals on the savannah so big?

As usual with evolutionary questions, there is no answer that is right or wrong, but more or less based on the knowledge we have today. The largest animals that live today are the whales that live in the sea, not on the savannahs. Why blue whales and elephants have become so large is probably due to the same cause: their food chains are extremely short.

Elephants graze grass and other vegetation that abounds in their habitats. Likewise, blue whales' food, krill, is found in huge quantities in their habitats.

BIG IS STRONG

The impressive size of their bodies alone allow elephants and blue whales to scare off potential predators. On islands where there are no predators, miniature species of elephants—pygmy elephants—have developed.

Did you know that...

. . . the ear of the African elephant is about three times larger than that of the Asian elephant? The African elephant's ear measures approximately 73 × 45 inches, while the Asian elephant's ear measures approximately 24 × 12 inches.

. . . a female elephant remains pregnant for 645 days (approximately 21 months)?

. . . the elephant is the only animal that has four knees?

. . . the scientific word for plant eaters is herbivores?

125

UNWELCOME GUESTS

Are we evolving—or are we invading?

An invasive alien species is a foreign species whose introduction and/or spread threatens biological diversity. This classic definition has recently been extended to include species that cause socioeconomic damage and harm to human health.

Alien species are species, subspecies, or lower taxa introduced outside their historical or contemporary natural ranges. The definition includes any part—gamete (sex cell), seed, egg, or other propagating part—that can sprout, survive, and give rise to new individuals.

Many native species are not invasive, but harmless, and many that arrive in Sweden do not even manage to establish themselves. Others may establish themselves, but do not succeed in spreading.

Approximately 2,000 nonnative species have been reported in Sweden. The vast majority are vascular plants and in a close second are arthropods. The list of foreign plant and animal species that become established in Sweden gets longer every year. The EPA has developed a blacklist of the species that threaten the native flora and fauna or are toxic. The preliminary list of "injurious species" includes 179 species.

Did you know that...

... the leopard slug came from southern Europe around the same time as the killer slug, which was about 30 years ago? They spread through purchased seedlings, and can be found almost everywhere and in great quantity. The leopard snail is an alien species that is not considered a pest. The killer slug, on the other hand, is an alien species regarded as a pest—that is, invasive.

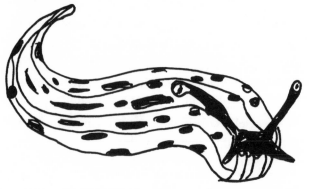

Some uninvited guests

CRAB

The Chinese mitten crab, which gets its name from its woolly front claws, is originally from temperate waters in the area between Vladivostok, Russia, and the Korean peninsula to the south of China, but has spread to Europe, the Mediterranean, and North America, probably via boat ballast tanks or being stuck on boat hulls. Because of its excellent ability to adapt to different environments in various rivers and lakes around the world, it is classified as one of the hundred most likely invasion species in the world.

In China, and in places where it is naturalized, the mitten crab lives in rivers and migrates to the salty seawater to reproduce. The larvae hatch in estuaries and live there for about 1.5 years, after which they migrate up the rivers. The species can cover long distances on land. Before it reaches sexual maturity, at about 5 years, it begins the journey back to the estuaries, where mating takes place in late autumn. The adult animals die some time after egg-laying. The mitten crab cannot propagate along the Baltic coast, likely because there is not a high enough salt content there. However, it is not impossible for the crab to multiply in the salty sea, outside Gothenburg (in the Göta River estuary).

The first discovery of the species outside of China was in Germany in 1912. It is now widespread in most of Europe's rivers and harbor areas, from the North Sea area down the Atlantic coast of Europe, including England and Ireland and into the Mediterranean Sea all the way to Turkey. The only European countries that do not have any reports of the presence of these crabs are the Faroe Islands, Iceland, and Greenland.

The first time the crabs were found in Sweden was in the 1930s. Since then they have been found along the coasts from the North Sea to the Baltic Sea and the Gulf of Bothnia. They are even found in Vänern and Lake Mälaren. They cannot reproduce in freshwater; thus, they are dependent on migration. In Vänern the crab's existence has declined, and no crabs (adult or juvenile) have been caught in the last two years.

The Spanish slug, *Arion vulgaris*, is also known as the "killer slug," as it eats other snails and under certain conditions is cannibalistic. It is 2.75–6 inches long, is gray-brown to reddish-brown, and has two longitudinal stripes on the body (visible mainly in young slugs). The species can be easily confused with other species of slugs, and to make a positive species identification, it is necessary to study the details inside the body. A single female can produce up to 400 eggs during her one-year lifetime.

The Spanish slug produces a lot of mucus and is tougher than most native slugs, which means that it is not attractive to predators. It has few natural enemies, but wild boars, badgers, hedgehogs, and blackbirds have been observed eating Spanish slugs. Some domestic ground beetles and predatory land snails, like a couple of the glass snails, occasionally eat their own eggs.

The Spanish slug appears in large groups and competes with native snail species. It eats native snail species and, in an area with a high incidence of Spanish slugs, may have a negative effect on soil biodiversity. In Dalby Forest, south of Skåne, for example, the plants' mercury levels have been destroyed by snail rampage.

BROOK TROUT

The brook trout, *Salvelinus fontinalis*, is not exactly an uninvited species in Sweden; as early as the 1880s, it was introduced to Swedish mountain waters for the first time, and it has subsequently spread across the country, but in many places releases have been unsuccessful.

131

Most releases implemented during the 1950s and 1960s were designed to improve fishing or replace previously unsuccessful releases of salmonids. The brook trout prefers cold, running water but also survives in the cold lakes of northern Sweden. It can also exist in warm water, provided that the oxygen content is high. The brook trout can handle extreme environmental conditions and can spread in water systems containing large obstacles, such as rivers with steep slopes. Unlike other introduced salmon species, this one successfully creates self-replicating species populations. The brook trout and the brown trout demonstrate a typical example of competition between two ecologically similar species, and the brook trout is known to out-compete the native trout.

AMERICAN LOBSTER

The American lobster, *Homarus americanus*, is very similar to the European lobster, *Homarus gammarus*. Because it is very difficult to morphologically confirm the species of newly found specimens, DNA testing is the only safe method for species identification. The two species have many similarities, such as reproduction, life cycle, habitat, and food preference, and therefore compete with each other. The introduction of the American lobster to Swedish coastal waters was noted outside Smögen's Harbor in November 2008. Four lobsters with typical characteristics of the American lobster were caught by a fisherman. With the aid of DNA analysis, it was confirmed that they were American lobsters. The lobsters probably had escaped from a marsh, where they were kept alive and fresh for sale. In Smögen there are several legitimate importers of live American lobsters.

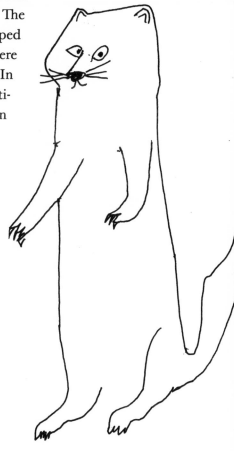

The American lobster's habitat utilization and foraging habits mirror those of the European lobster. It is therefore likely that the two species are competing for the same food and space.

Some other guests are:
→ Giant hogweed
→ Warty comb jelly
→ German cockroach
→ Mink
→ Pacific oyster
→ Elm disease

Is the raccoon dog in Sweden?

The first confirmed sighting of the raccoon dog in Sweden was outside Arjeplog in the autumn of 1947. Additional confirmed raccoon dog sightings were in Svappavaara in 1972, Pajala in 1983, and Vittangi in 1989, all in the county of Norrbotten. The first confirmed discovery in Västerbotten County was in Lövånger in 1989. But it was only in the mid-2000s that the raccoon dog population truly started to take off. A likely reason for the increased activity is that those years had mild winters. The first regeneration of the species on Swedish soil was confirmed in 2006. In 2009, an old raccoon dog was shot just outside of Umeå, which was the southernmost discovery. There is absolutely no evidence that there has ever been a raccoon dog in central or southern Sweden.

A SURE SIGN

The surest sign of the raccoon dog is its dung piles, because it leaves its droppings in piles in a way that no domestic animals do.

The raccoon dog can also be separated from the badger through its tracks. The raccoon dog has four toes on each foot, while the badger has five.

The raccoon dog, *Nyctereutes procyonoides*, is a small dog-relative that cannot bark. Its natural range is Japan and eastern China, from the Amur River to Vietnam. In body color, shape, and size, it resembles the badger; however, it has longer limbs and a hanging, bushy tail. Like the badger, it has black-and-white facial markings (a black mask), evoking the raccoon even more.

In the early 1900s, the species was introduced to fur farms in European Russia, and also in parts of Finland. The resulting coat was called Siberian raccoon or Ussuri raccoon. Russian farmers maintained the raccoon dogs, and they established themselves well and spread quickly. The Russians also released raccoon dogs deliberately, to hunt them for their fur. Nowadays they are found throughout European Russia and in Finland, the Baltics, Poland, and Germany, and some a bit farther south.

Ecologically, the raccoon dog inhabits the same biotopes as foxes and badgers; it digs a den. It is omnivorous and also eats berries and fruit. Although the raccoon dog is a canine, it is not at all a good predator. It lives mostly on small rodents, berries, fruits, nuts, and various small animals. In the fall, it eats itself quite fat in order to hibernate through the winter. It prefers areas with dense, often damp undergrowth. The raccoon dog is a shy animal that lives in the shadows and avoids being detected by humans whenever possible. Its specialty is to hide or make itself invisible by becoming motionless, making it very difficult to spot. Ground-nesting birds are exposed to increased predation in areas where the

135

species is established. The raccoon dog was found to be a carrier of rabies without being affected itself. It can probably also spread fox tapeworm.

It was feared that the raccoon dog would expand in Sweden, partly through migration from Finland, and from the farms that existed in Sweden. These fears have so far proven unfounded. Nobody knows how many raccoon dogs are in Sweden today, or really even where they are. While the chances are extremely high that they are inaccurate, isolated reports of raccoon dogs pop up now and then from all over Sweden, except the mountains.

Since the raccoon dog does not belong to the natural Swedish animal world, and they are not desired to become established there, controlled raccoon dog hunting is allowed year-round.

Many reported discoveries of raccoon dogs have actually been badgers, but they are not really very similar: the badger is chubby and has short legs, a short tail, and an elongated head with contrasting stripes of black and white along the head; the raccoon dog's masked head has a pointed, fox-like snout and it is not as contrastingly colored as a badger's.

❧ MYTH ❧

Old folklore indicates that you should stuff coal, crisp bread, or something similar in your boots if you are out walking in the badger-rich regions. Previously it was thought that a badger particularly loved attacking people's legs, and would not let go until it heard a crunching sound!

But badgers are not bone crushers; they are omnivores that feed on such delicious delights as earthworms, snails, rodents, birds, eggs, reptiles, frogs, grasses, and berries.

MORE THAN
DANGEROUS

THE MOST TOXIC: POISONOUS AND SINGLE

What is the most toxic?

There are lots of different toxic animals, and there is no serious research that has identified one species or the other as the world's most toxic. Not even the *Guinness Book of World Records* weighs in on this. However, it does list the top species in specific groups. For example, the most venomous snake is a sea serpent named *Hydrophis melanocephalus* and the most venomous land snake is an Australian taipan called the fierce snake, *Oxyuranus microlepidotus*.

The data on which spider is the most venomous varies greatly, but according to *Guinness,* it is the Brazilian wandering spider, *Phoneutria fera*, that is considered to have the strongest venom of all spiders.

Other venomous spiders of note are the Australian redback spider, *Latrodectus hasselti*, the Sydney funnel-web spiders, *Atrax robustus* and *Hadronyche infensa*, and the red-headed mouse spider, *Missulena occatoria*. In addition, there is the Sri Lankan ornamental tarantula, *Poecilotheria fasciata*, which is perhaps the most dangerous tarantula. In North America there are a couple of venomous species: the brown recluse, *Loxosceles reclusa*, and the black widow, *Latrodectus mactans*. The Mediterranean black widow, *Latrodectus tredecimguttatus*, is a toxic spider found in southern Europe.

Scorpion toxicity is unclear and varies with different authors' views. According to some writers, a healthy person could never die from a scorpion sting, while others argue that a person who gets stung by, for example, the Baja California bark scorpion, *Centruroides exilicauda*, must be treated with antidotes within 8 hours or it will result in death. Other species mentioned as the most toxic are the North African fat-tailed scorpion, *Androctonus australis*, and the Palestine yellow scorpion, *Leiurus quinquestriatus*, which is also called the deathstalker.

EAT OR BE EATEN

Being able to defend and avoid becoming another's food is essential for life, but one must also be able to get hold of food in order to survive. Defense can be accomplished in many ways. One can assume threatening postures, make intimidating gestures, play dead, have a protective armor, camouflage, or be toxic (or at least appear toxic).

Many animals produce their venom themselves with the help of specialized cells. Other animals become poisonous by eating toxic animals or plants. This is

142

common among both insects and sea animals. Toxins are often complex in composition and consist of a variety of substances, from simple organic compounds to complex enzymes. Different toxins affect different parts of the victim: the nervous system, heart function, blood system, or local tissue.

Did you know that...

... there is a snake, a sharp-nosed viper, found in Southeast Asia called the hundred pacer, *Deinagkistrodon acutus*? That's right; according to legend, once you are bitten by one, you will only walk 100 more steps. Nor is the common death adder, *Acanthophis antarcticus*, a completely harmless snake! It lives in Australia and New Guinea, and it is considered one of the world's most venomous land snakes.

OFFENSIVELY OR DEFENSIVELY VENEMOUS

Put simply, one can say that there are two types of toxic animals. One type uses poison as a defense against its attackers, while the other obtains food by using venom. In animals that live in the ocean, most toxicity fills a defensive need. Venomous snakes, on the other hand, make use of venom as an offensive weapon. Some animals, such as scorpions, use toxins as both defense and attack weapons.

143

In Egypt, shark attacks . . .

In late 2010, it was reported from Egypt that sharks were attacking people at the resort of Sharm el-Sheikh.

For a time it was believed that the shark that was terrorizing people was the oceanic whitetip shark, a cosmopolitan species that lives in tropical and temperate seas. The whitetip averages 8 feet long, but the longest has been measured at about 13 feet. The highest recorded weight is 368 pounds and the oldest known specimen was 22 years old. It is easily recognized by its rounded and white-tipped pectoral fins—hence its common name.

But when it was caught, it turned out to be a mako shark. (Of course, it is also speculated that it could have been a great white shark, which is always depicted as a human-devouring monster whenever a shark fin is visible near a beach.)

The mako shark is about the same size as the whitetip shark, and is thus able to take on large prey. Considering the research, though, makos are more likely to provoke anxiety than cause real danger to humans. However, they can be potentially dangerous and they are known to have attacked swimmers and boats, unprovoked. They are also likely the fastest of all sharks.

Makos have about the same cosmopolitan distribution and way of life as whitetips. Generally, though, makos dwell at a depth of 325–500 feet, while whitetips swim at 0–750 feet. This means that makos are quite rarely in the nearshore waters, especially compared to whitetips. The mako is slightly more common than the whitetip, but it is still categorized on the International Union

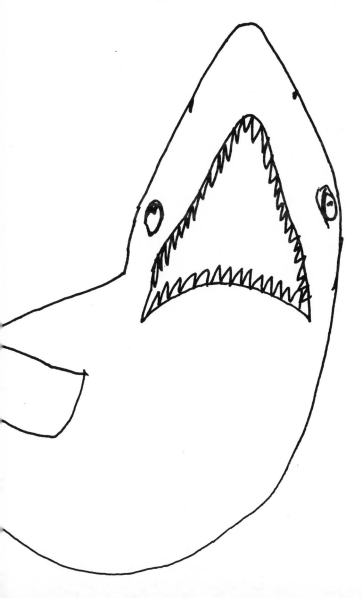

for Conservation of Nature (IUCN) Red List as near threatened.

Why these sharks attacked humans at Sharm el-Sheikh is still being debated. One hypothesis is that a ship with livestock tossed animals that died into the sea, which lured sharks to the area. This is possible. From a shark's perspective, there is not a big difference between a floating cow and a snorkeling man.

A more likely hypothesis is that sharks were lured by feeding for photography purposes. While this is clearly prohibited in the Red Sea, it is known to have occurred anyway. To do this, a photographer holds a large fish in his hand and the shark comes to take a bite; thus, fine underwater images can be taken of sharks attacking prey.

SHARK FACTS

Sometimes a whitetip strays to Sweden. In 2004 a dead specimen was found at Skredsvik in Gullmarn in Bohuslän, far north of where it normally travels.

The whitetip is one of the ground sharks, and that includes some of the best-known and most-common sharks: the bull shark, the tiger shark, and the blue shark. Several species can grow very large, with the largest of them all being the tiger shark, which can be over 24 feet long.

All sharks have round eyes, and their pectoral fins are located just behind the five gill openings. Most species give birth to live young.

Sharks, like rays, have no bone formation and are part of the class of cartilaginous fish. There are nearly

400 different species of sharks and most live in the sea, but a few species of sharks do well even in freshwater.

Sharks, unlike other fish, have no swim bladder to keep them afloat in the water. Therefore, they have to move constantly to refrain from sinking to the bottom.

Almost all sharks have an elongated, streamlined body. The skin is covered by small, toothlike scales that feel like sandpaper. The so-called sharkskin swimsuit was common among competitive swimmers before it was banned in 2010.

Statistically, it is highly unlikely to be attacked by a shark, and much more likely to die of sunstroke on the beach. A dozen species are considered to have the ability to attack people with serious consequences, and some have demonstrated the ability to kill, such as the white shark, the tiger shark, the bull shark, and the mako shark.

Sharks replenish their teeth constantly. Tooth replacement rates differ between species and depend on age, diet, seasonality, and water temperature. Most sharks replace only a few teeth at a time, but some lose entire rows at once.

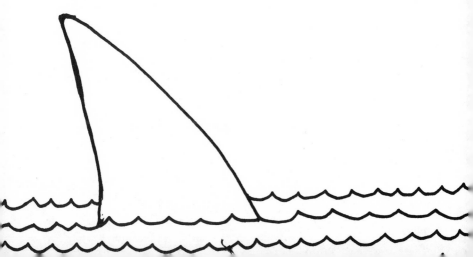

. . . and in Thailand, the toxic "jellyfish" made headlines . . .

With some regularity, articles about dangerous jellyfish fill the newspapers, but some of them are not jellyfish. The animals that cause a number of these annual tragedies are the so-called box jellyfish, a class among the Cnidarians.

There are about 40 known species of box jellyfish. They are easily identified by their cubic bodies with four tentacles or tentacle groups—one in each corner. Knowledge of the species is generally considered very incomplete. But we do know that some species have very dangerous stinging cells. In the Australian and Asian waters, there are some species that can be deadly. The sea wasp, *Chironex fleckeri*, is considered the most dangerous, and is reported to have caused hundreds, some say thousands, of deaths in the 1900s and 2000s. They have a bluish, translucent, bell-shaped body with four sides. From each corner hang up to 15 tentacles that can reach nearly 10 feet long. Each tentacle can have upwards of 5,000 nematocysts (stinging cells).

When it comes to true jellyfish, there is probably no species that is fatally venomous. A troublesome species is the Atlantic sea nettle, *Chrysaora quinquecirrha*, found in temperate and tropical seas. The strength of the venom varies from moderate to severe, but it is never potent enough to kill a human being (except by an allergic reaction).

In Swedish waters, only the lion's mane jellyfish, *Cyanea capillata*, stings significantly. It is not fatal to

humans, although it can cause discomfort and pain.

THROW IT AWAY

If you see a box jellyfish swimming toward you, it is possible to lift it up and throw it away. Lift from above the globular "head." There are no poisonous tentacles there.

Stingrays, stonefish, and lionfish

At least a thousand species of fish are known to have, or be likely to have, a toxin-producing device, or contain toxins scattered throughout some tissue. Stingrays, of the family Dasyatidae, are found in all temperate and warm seas. They have one or more venomous, barbed tags in the tail. Stingrays easily lie buried in the sand in shallow water. If you happen to trample carelessly, you can easily catch a thorn in the foot.

Some other venomous fish also lie buried, including weevers (genus *Trachinus*) and stargazers (*Uranoscopidae*). The camouflaged stonefish, *Synanceia verrucosa*—sometimes regarded as the world's most venomous fish—stabs attackers with venomous spines when attacked.

The red lionfish, *Pterois volitans,* lives in a coral reef environment and has bright colors with fins resembling

151

bird feathers, with spines that are connected to venom glands.

THE WORLD'S MOST DANGEROUS MEAL

There are about 120 species of puffer fish, of the family Tetraodontidae, and some of them contain the poison tetradotoxin (TTX), which is one of the most potent animal toxins we know. It is considered to be 25 times as strong as curare. The poison is also found in other fish, so in total there are about 75 species of fish that contain TTX. In Japan the pufferfish is called *fugu* (river pig) and is cooked for a dish that has been called the world's most dangerous meal, or a gastronomic version of Russian roulette. Cooking fugu is considered an art form, and fugu chefs undergo extensive training before they are licensed to cook it. Among gourmands, the liver is most highly praised, and it is the most toxic part of fugu (but it is now banned by law to serve). The number of deaths has decreased, but the Japanese still have a saying regarding this particular gamble: "Yesterday he and I ate fugu. Today I carry his coffin."

WEEVERS—SWEDISH MONSTER

The greater weever, *Trachinus draco*, is Sweden's most, and possibly only, venomous fish. It lives in the North Sea coastal areas at depths of 15–80 feet, where it is buried in the sandy floor. The fish's head and first dorsal fin are usually just above the sea floor while it looks for suitable prey. With seven venomous spines, the greater weever can attack suitable prey and spread its venom, which causes temporary paralysis and renders the victim unable to escape.

152

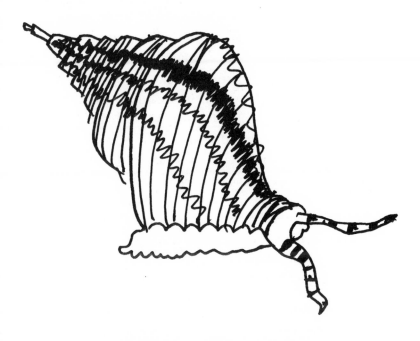

CHEMICAL WAR MACHINES

Some gastropods, like *Tonna galea*, have the ability to secrete very acidic solutions containing approximately 3 percent sulfuric acid and other toxic components. It is believed that the shell uses this to dissolve the stony armor of starfish, sea urchins, and small crustaceans, which are its prey. The liquid is also used for defensive purposes.

Cone snails, of the family Conidae, represent perhaps the most amazing and intricate chemical war machines nature created. They are predators and each has a fleshy, long, hollow radular tooth with which it attacks its prey (fish, mollusks, and marine worms). The tooth is connected to a venom gland, and the prey is

paralyzed very quickly after attacked. The most dangerous of these snails, *Conus geographus*, from the Indian
Ocean, has caused 20 reported human deaths.

TOXIC ECHINODERMS

Sea urchins, of the class Echinoidea, bear pedicellariae, which are found between the spines. Pedicellariae
are claw-like structures that form gripping tongs, and
are 0.04–0.15 inches long. Pedicellariae act as effective
defense agents, and in some species they are equipped
with poison glands. When the sea urchin is attacked
the venom is released from the tip of the gripping tongs
and is injected into the aggressor. A sea urchin species
found from the west coast of Africa to Japan, *Toxopneus-
tes pileolus*, is feared for its venom.

THE OCTOPUS

There are some squid species that are toxic, even so
toxic that we could be affected. The posterior salivary
glands of the common octopus, *Octopus vulgaris*, found
in the eastern Atlantic and Mediterranean seas, secrete
a strongly acidic solution that is toxic to crabs, causing the crab viscera to melt down. People who have
been attacked by this octopus usually experience severe
pain, but recover quickly. The blue-ringed octopuses,
Hapalochlaena maculosa and *H. lunulata,* which exist
along Australia's coasts, are common in tide pools.
These beautifully colored, small beings (4–8 inches
long) have remarkably large posterior salivary glands
containing a highly potent neurotoxin. This toxin is
believed to have caused occasional human deaths.

154

... AND ON LAND

AMPHIBIANS AND POISON DARTS

Many frogs and toads protect themselves using toxic skin secretions. Most are not particularly dangerous for us, but some, like the poison dart frogs of the family Dendrobatidae, secrete some of the most potent biological toxins known to man. With their small size and crisp, spectacular colors, combined with their extreme toxicity, the poison dart frogs create a captivating animal group. The toxic liquid is dispensed in connection with danger or stress. A batrachotoxin is one of the most deadly venoms. From the Colombian black-legged dart frog, *Phyllobates bicolor*, as little as 0.2 milligrams is enough to kill a normal-size man.

WITH A VENOMOUS BITE

It was long thought that there were only two species among all lizards that were venomous: the Gila monster, *Heloderma suspectum*, and the Mexican bearded lizard, *Heloderma horridum*. Relatively recently, we learned that even the Komodo dragon, *Varanus komodoensis*, has a venomous bite. The Gila monster and Mexican bearded lizard advertise their toxicity with striking coloration. Their venom glands are located in the lower jaw, and chewing movements disperse the powerful venom through grooves in the lower and upper teeth.

The Komodo dragon has large venom glands in the lower jaw which open when the jaw is clenched tightly, like when it is around a deer's leg. The sharp teeth create deep wounds, allowing the venom to enter the animal's bloodstream.

Of the nearly 3,000 species of snake, only about 10 percent are toxic, but these are the ones we usually hear about. The Australian inland taipan, *Oxyuranus microlepidotus* (formerly *Parademansia microlepidota*), is, according to *Guinness*, the most venomous land snake in the world. The inland taipan's venom has been determined to be four times as strong as the coastal taipan's, *Oxyuranus scutellatus*, and nine times as strong as that of the tiger snake, *Notechis scutatus*, which is also from

Australia. The Southeast Asian kraits (genus *Bungarus*) also contain a very powerful poison. The only snakes outside Australia and Asia with a toxin comparable to the kraits' are the North American Eastern coral snake, *Micrurus fulvius*, and the African boomslang, *Dispholidus typus*.

EATING DANGEROUS INSECTS

There are no dangerously poisonous birds, but there are some species we should watch out for. At least three species of *Pitohui* (*Pitohui dichrous*, *P. kirhocephalus*, and *P. ferrugineus*), should be avoided, by both touching and eating. They are all in New Guinea. A neurotoxin called homobatrachotoxin, found in the plumage and skin, causes numbness and tingling in parts that come in contact with the bird.

Another bird, the blue-capped ifrita, *Ifrita kowaldi*, which is also found in New Guinea, has toxic alkaloids in its plumage and skin. And, in Australia and New Guinea, there is the little shrikethrush, *Colluricincla megarhyncha*, which can also cause problems.

POISONOUS SHREWS

There are only a few species of mammals that are toxic. The most familiar is the platypus, *Ornithorhynchus anatinus*, of which males have a venomous spine on the hind legs. The venom is painful, but not lethal to humans.

In Sweden there is the Eurasian water shrew, *Neomys fodiens*, which has venomous saliva that is used to paralyze prey. This allows it to take down large prey, such as frogs.

In addition, there are two species of solenodon, *Solenodon cubanus* in Cuba and *S. paradoxus* in Haiti, that have poisonous bites. Three shrews of the genus *Blarina* also have venomous bites. The greater slow loris, *Nycticebus coucang*, has glands on the inside of the elbows that produce a toxin that smells like sweaty socks. It covers its young with the toxin as protection against predators, and adults can produce a venomous bite through the lower front teeth.

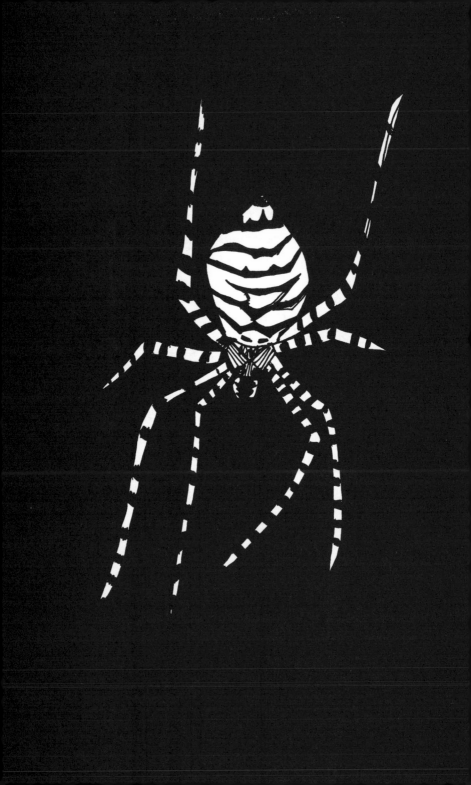

TERRIBLY DANGEROUS COLORS

Why are poisonous animals often colorful?

Colors play an important role in the lives of many organisms, especially in the animal kingdom. The colors are usually not arbitrary for each animal, but often have survival value. Some animals display colors to blend in with their surroundings, while others would rather have colors that are visible. The strategy need not be the same throughout the animal's development, either. With insects, larvae and fully formed insects do not require the same color scale.

By having clear and sharply contrasting colors, some animals signal that they are not tasty, or even poisonous, and can thus avoid attack.

Typical combinations are black and yellow or black and red. Sometimes these colors are combined, and sometimes white is involved. This color palette is usually referred to as aposematic coloration.

There are many examples of animals that display a yellow-black coloration either to blend in with the surroundings or to be seen. The species with warning colors of yellow and black that you will probably think of first is the wasp, which is venomous.

Other examples of toxic bugs with these colors are the wasp spider, *Argiope bruennichi*, the cinnabar moth, *Tyria jacobaeae*, and several species of ladybugs, of the family Coccinellidae. Many bumblebees (*Bombus* spp.) can also be included in this category. The wasp spider has venom that dissolves the prey caught in its web. The cinnabar moth lives solely on ragwort, *Senecio jacobaea*. Horses can get liver damage from the toxin contained in ragwort.

Finally, bumblebees do not burn us; it only feels this way when the venom is injected into the skin.

Did you know that...

... the field digger wasp, *Mellinus arvensis*, is a specialist in taking flies? It injects the fly with a venom that is not lethal, but paralyzing. The immobile fly later becomes food for field digger wasp larvae when the eggs hatch.

Some insects in red and black:

→ Minstrel bug (true bug)
→ Red-and-black bug (true bug)
→ Firebug (true bug)
→ Smoky moths (butterflies)
→ Ladybug (beetle)

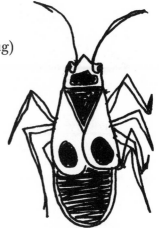

The most frequently emerging question related to black-and-red insects involves the identification of three species of true bugs, "lice," which are also beetle-like and which can appear in large numbers. These three species can be easily confused with yet another true bug.

Of these four species, the minstrel bug is the easiest to identify. It is regularly colored in long black-and-red streaks.

The other three species are irregularly colored. Among them, the red-and-black bug has a round white spot on the wings, which rest on the membranous section.

The firebug has a black triangle on the back and a black shield on the neck, and the wings have round black spots. The similar Rhopalinae have red centers (shields) on the back triangle, their neck shields have two black spots, and their side wings have black rectangles.

163

. . . the ladybug can secrete a yellow fluid from the leg joints that is both toxic and foul-tasting?

BATESIAN MIMICRY

There are other, nontoxic species that benefit from mimicking toxic species. A nontoxic species resembling a toxic one benefits by avoiding predators, such as birds, that have learned to avoid the toxic species. This tinctorial mimicry is called Batesian mimicry, after the British natural historian Henry Bates.

Among the harmless species that are designed in yellow and black are, for example, hoverflies (of the family Syrphidae), many clearwings, like the hornet moth, *Sesia apiformis*, and the larvae of the alder moth, *Acronicta alni*, and the broom moth, *Melanchra pisi*.

POISONOUS MOTHS

Among the Lepidoptera, the poisonous species are almost exclusively moths, and even then more frequently the larvae than the fully formed moths. The toxic species' larvae are often heavily coated and the hairs are connected to toxin-producing mini-glands. When touched, the hairs are easily broken off and stuck in the victim's skin. The fox moth, *Macrothylacia rubi*, is an example of this.

The monarch butterfly, *Danaus plexippus*, is a common, everyday butterfly that is poisonous, but it does not produce any toxins itself. Monarch larvae feed on poisonous milkweed. The venom is stored up in the caterpillar's bodily fluids with no detrimental effect on either the larva or the fully formed butterfly. A bird that eats a monarch quickly realizes that the butterfly is poisonous. The bird is saved when the venom stimulates an emetic center in the brain, causing it to quickly get rid of the poison.

The bombardier beetle, *Brachinus crepitans*, has a unique chemical defense. When attacked, it emits an explosive gas that is directed toward the aggressor. The temperature of the gas can reach over 200°F, and the firing is audible even to us. The attacker can be bombarded several times in rapid succession with the gas.

How social are wasps?

They vary: there are social wasps, and solitary ones. The solitary wasps do not live in communities and have no working caste system, only females and males. The females build their nests of mud or utilize existing cavities in wood where they lay their eggs. Each egg is provided with an insect that the female paralyzed with her venom. When the eggs hatch, the paralyzed insects become food for the wasp larvae.

Among the social wasps, there are females, males, and workers. The females and workers, which are sterile females, have stingers. Most species live in fairly large communities for one year.

Some social wasp species do not build their own nests, but use other species' nests. Therefore, they have no need of a working caste system—they let the host species do all the work.

MANY SPECIES

Wasps have a worldwide distribution and there are about 3,250 different species. Most species are found in both tropical and subtropical areas. Only 12 of the social wasp species care for their own offspring. Of the solitary wasps, there are 38 species in Sweden. In addition, there is a species belonging to the paper wasps.

THE LIFE OF A SOCIAL WASP

The wasp female, the queen, that was conceived the previous fall, arrives in the spring after having wintered in a protected location. She begins almost immediately to

166

build a new nest with a frame of chewed wood. Inside the new wooden house, she builds cells and lays an egg in each one. From the eggs hatch larvae that the queen rears with nectar and meat in various forms (mostly insects). After a few weeks the larvae pupate, and after another week the pupae hatch. The individuals that hatch are sterile females, and destined to be workers. The workers now take over the queen's efforts to build the nest and feed the larvae. From now on, the queen concentrates solely on the production of eggs. If it is a warm and not too humid summer, the nest can house a large number of individuals. Toward the end of the season, when daylight is shorter, the queen gives birth to individuals of both sexes. The newly hatched queens will then mate with males from other nests, and after mating, the female goes into hibernation. These are the new queens that will form new communities the following year, while the old queens, workers, and males will die.

NEST

The nest is built of wood, scraped from dead trees, which is chewed with saliva to a pulp. It may be constructed hanging under a roof, in branches, in underground burrows, or in hollow trees. The nest consists of slabs of hexagonal cells in several tiers and is usually surrounded by a casing.

FRUIT LOVER

Wasps are predators and take prisoners, including the insect larvae that they feed to their own larvae. Which

168

insect species they prey upon most depends on their immediate surroundings. The adults willingly drink nectar, however, and sugary saliva that is emitted by their own larvae, but they also eat fruit, meat, and fish. In late summer wasps often concentrate around ripe fruits and other sweets.

Wasps have biting mouthparts and a short, wide tongue. With it, they lick the nectar from flowers where nectar is easy to access. The rose family, carrot family, and coneflower plants have wasp-friendly flowers with easily accessible nectar.

Wasps love to visit common fruit and berry plants, such as apples, pears, plums, cherries, strawberries, raspberries, and blackberries, which are all pollinated largely by the wasps.

THE DEEPEST—GROUND WASPS

The wasps that place their nests in underground burrows are called ground wasps.

Of Swedish wasps, only three species nest in the ground. They are called the plain, south, and red wasp, and are the most common wasp species. These three species also build nests above ground and often in human proximity. When the nest is placed in the ground and we tread nearby, this creates vibrations in the ground, and of course also in the nest. This raises the natural defense instinct of wasps to immediately investigate and ideally chase away that which brought disruption. This almost never occurs with nests located above ground.

The hornet is the biggest wasp in Europe. It is easily recognized by the orange color of the abdomen and the reddish areas high on the head. Despite, or perhaps because of, its size, it is the least aggressive of the Swedish wasps.

There are many legends, myths, and stories about the European hornet, and it is often portrayed as prone to attack. The truth is that you have to provoke it properly to get it to attack.

The hornet is a typical woodland species. It often chooses a cavity in an old tree as a home.

Which is the most dangerous animal in Sweden?

Many do not see the difference between a bee (*Apis mellifera*, Western honeybee) and a wasp, of the family Vespidae. Therefore, it can be difficult to know which insect attacked. A wasp can attack several times because the stinger does not have barbs. Tambiets (which include bees) have barbs on the stinger (and sometimes across the whole bee), and these remain stuck after the attack. Since the stinger usually remains in the victim, the bee dies after stinging.

The venom of a tambiet is very complex and consists of more than 40 different substances. Wasp venom contains some of the same substances as those found in bees. As a hypersensitivity can easily evolve towards

170

certain components of the venom, domestic bees and wasps likely cause more deaths among people in Sweden than any other venomous animals. Wasp and tambiets are two of Sweden's most dangerous animals.

While the tick is a very dangerous animal that spreads several diseases, we really do not know how many people fall ill every year as a result of tick encounters.

Did you know that...

... in stinging wasps, called Aculeata, the egg-laying tube (ovipositor) communicates with a toxin gland? The toxin is complex and consists of a number of amines, peptides, and proteins that have a strong pain-inducing effect.

POISONOUS PLANTS

Why are some plants poisonous?

Plants often have different built-in defenses against being eaten by insect larvae, primarily, but also by grazing animals. Barbs and thorns are just some of several deterrents, but the most effective are the chemical contents of the plants. These substances can cause other living organisms, including humans, serious injury if swallowed, or even through skin contact.

Most poisonous plants in Sweden are instinctively rejected by grazing animals. This applies, for example, to buttercups, *Ranunculus* spp., which are toxic when fresh, but not in the dried state, such as hay. Even dried ragwort, *Senecio jacobaea*, contains several toxic alkaloids that can be dangerous for cattle if too much of it is mixed into the hay. Too much can also lead to liver injuries in horses.

173

The substances in plants can be divided into a number of groups according to their toxic contents. In addition to the following groups of substances, there are other substances in different parts of the plant kingdom of unknown constitution, but of known toxicity. Substances that cause skin and mucosal irritation are found in plants such as hogweed, American castor, and poppies.

Alkaloids are nitrogenous, basic plant substances. They are often very dangerous toxins, and are found in many parts of the plant kingdom, but are especially common among the potato plants, poppy plants, and umbelliferous plants (such as hemlock).

Glycosides are chemical compounds of sugars and other elements. They are common in the plant kingdom and are often highly toxic.

Saponins are a type of glycoside that have surfactant effects and may cause vomiting and diarrhea.

Volatile oils are a group of substances that can cause skin irritation and blistering, as well as kidney and nerve damage.

SOCRATES AND HEMLOCK

There are a lot of really poisonous plants in Sweden. Most familiar is perhaps the most highly toxic, poison hemlock, *Conium maculatum*, which is associated with the philosophy of one of history's greatest thinkers, Socrates, who lived in 400 BC. At 70 years old, he was brought to trial on charges of disdain for the state's belief in the gods, and exerting a harmful influence on the youth. Socrates was sentenced to death,

174

and emptied without hesitation a poisoned cup, which contained hemlock. Poison hemlock contains the alkaloid coniine, and the taste is said to be very unpleasant, so the risk of accidental ingestion is considered remote.

Burning bushes and dead cows

DEADLY NIGHTSHADE (*ATROPA BELLADONNA*)

This plant is very poisonous. It contains atropine. Severe poisonings have occurred in medical use and in abusive uses.

Symptoms: dry mouth, facial flushing, palpitations, dizziness, wide pupils, blurred vision, and hallucinations. In serious cases, possibly even loss of consciousness and seizures.

NORTHERN WOLFSBANE (*ACONITUM LYCOCTONUM*)

Northern wolfsbane is highly toxic. Especially the seeds and roots, which contain aconitine. Severe poisonings and even deaths have occurred in medical use and in confusion with edible roots.

Symptoms: can come on suddenly, within one hour, with burning sensations in the mouth and throat, vomiting, diarrhea, salivation, cold sweats, tingling, visual disturbances, heart rhythm disorders, convulsions, and respiratory paralysis.

BURNING BUSH (*DICTAMNUS ALBUS*)

The plants, especially the seed pods, contain an oil that is irritating to the skin, especially if the skin is exposed to sunlight (a so-called phototoxic reaction). Poisoning by eating the plant is not known.

Symptoms: burn-like symptoms to severe skin irritation and blisters. Symptoms may persist for weeks, possibly even scarring and darkening the skin.

176

LILY OF THE VALLEY (*CONVALLARIA MAJALIS*)

The flowers and leaves, especially, contain substances that are irritating and can affect the heart. Severe poisoning is uncommon. Ingestion of flower water is harmless.

Symptoms: abdominal discomfort. In serious cases, possibly cardiac arrhythmias.

THE ENGLISH YEW (*TAXUS BACCATA*)

Includes toxins and an irritating oil. Only the red pulp of the fruit is safe, with everything else being toxic. Ingestion of pine needles and chewed seeds involves poisoning risk. Serious poisonings are rare in humans. In 2001, six cows died in Sweden after someone threw cuttings of spruce, arborvitae, and yew trees in their pasture.

Symptoms: abdominal discomfort. In serious cases, possibly even heart failure.

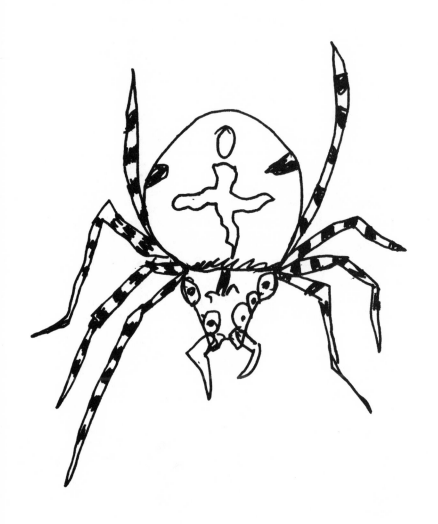

SPIDER, SPIDER ON THE WALL

Are there any poisonous spiders in Sweden?

Of all spiders, about 99.2 percent are venomous, but only about 200 species contain a toxicity that is problematic for humans. The venom of most spiders is intended for insects and used to stun prey. It is likely that there are no dangerous spiders in Sweden. Poisonous spiders are, however, in many hiking stories, especially in older literature.

The female water spider is large and is known to be fierce. The same is true of female raft spiders, European garden spiders, and some other orb-weaver spiders. Being bitten by one of these would certainly be felt, but a bite will take a very unfortunate turn if the chelicerae (mouth parts) penetrate the skin. It is through chelicerae that venom enters the prey. These usually contain dagger-like or claw-like tips, and the poison gland, which is located inside the body, is discharged through a channel in the tip. In older books you can read that the yellow sac spider, *Cheiracanthium puncto-rium*, (of the family Miturgidae) can be fatal to Swedes. To my ears, this sounds very unlikely. It is a rare species in Sweden and is found in about 15 locales in Öland and Gotland. It could be said that in order to be bitten by it, one must be in Öland and Gotland in a swamp with large grasshoppers and crawling around on all fours in the middle of the night. This basically leaves only on-call biologists and a handful of others as potential victims!

A WIDOW WITH A BITE

The most studied spider venom is in the black widow, *Latrodectus mactans*, which is found in the United States. This venom contains a protein called latrotoxin. The bite can pass unnoticed for a few minutes or possibly be perceived as a stabbing pain. Subsequently, pain radiates from the bite site. The pain spreads to the muscles of the trunk, arms, and legs. The victim generally becomes anxious, trembles, and may have difficulty breathing, and sometimes experiences a sensation of dying. Symptoms reach a maximum intensity 6–12 hours after the bite. The bite of the black widow is rarely fatal, although it is associated with severe pain.

Did you know that...

... especially in winter, the spider is actually an important part of the diet for many of Sweden's species? Also, summer spiders are a major part of the diet for the so-called insect-eating birds. So, to call these birds only insectivores is actually a bit misleading.

... spiders are egg-laying, and the eggs are laid in small bundles of silk, called sacs?

... some spiders carry these sacs around until the eggs hatch?

... there are about 42,000 known spider species in the world, 705 of which are found in Sweden?

... spiders can only consume liquid food? The spider sucks the insides out of its prey.

The largest arachnid is a scorpion. This nocturnal predator is well known for its toxicity. The body is divided into a thorax and an abdomen, ending in a tail with a venomous stinger at the tip. The toxin is formed in two sacs as glands that each sting separately. All scorpions are venomous, but only a small number represent a danger to us. These are found mainly in warmer regions. In the eastern Mediterranean countries of Europe, the yellow scorpion, *Mesobuthus gibbosus*, can be found, and this can cause a serious sting.

What are ticks good for?

Short answer: they are simply very good at just being ticks.

A little longer of an answer: the tick exists for its own sake, like all other species, and success in this regard is very much about the ability to survive and reproduce. And the tick has great success with this. From a human perspective, perhaps a little too good, but humans do not care much for the tick. The tick has found its ecological niche, where it is extremely successful. In addition, it has several other functions:

→ The tick is food for many animals, including birds, frogs, toads, lizards, spiders, and ground beetles.

→ The tick transmits bacteria, viruses, and microorganisms from a host animal to another. The tick is probably important for the regulation of the host animal populations.

→ The tick hosts several parasitic species that attack the genus *Ixodes*. *Ixodiphagus (Hunterellus) hookeri*, in the parasite family Encyrtidae, is the most well known of them.

183

Is the vulture an agent of a foreign power?

A griffon vulture that found its way into Saudi Arabia was arrested (according to the Swedish newspaper *Aftonbladet* on January 4, 2011):

"He is suspected of being an Israeli spy. The vulture had a transmitter on the foot that was labeled *Tel Aviv University*. This suggests that it is part of a research project where the birds' migration patterns are studied. But in the area where the vulture was taken, they are convinced that it is a Zionist conspiracy, wrote the Israeli newspaper *Haaretz*.

"Arabic websites speculated that the bird was trained by the Israeli intelligence service Mossad. Conspiracy theories about Mossad are not uncommon in the area. Last month, the governor of the Egyptian Sinai Peninsula claimed that it may be Israel who released the deadly shark that attacked tourists at Sharm El-Sheikh."

A LITTLE GREEN
ON IT, THANKS

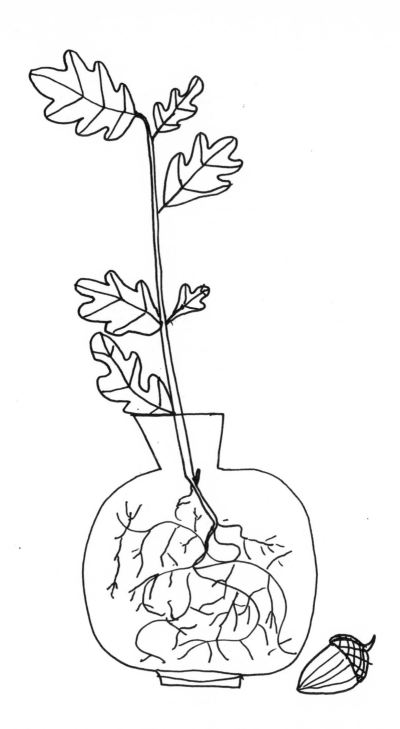

COME FORTH, SHRUB

How is an oak tree made?

Start with at least a dozen acorns, preferably even more for a greater chance that something will grow. Place the acorns in a bowl and set them on a windowsill. Cover them completely with water and add more water when needed, because the acorns must not become dry. After 3–6 weeks the acorns should crack a bit at the ends, and if you are lucky, small white sprouts will begin to creep out. When the germ is showing, it is extra important that it does not become dry. When the germ grows to be about half an inch long, you can place it in a vase. Position the acorn standing upright with the germ (the prospective root) down. It must now stand with the germ submerged in water at all times. It may take up to 3–6 weeks more before the actual oak sapling slowly springs up from the acorn. Then it can grow quickly, and when it gets its first true leaves, you can plant the whole plant in soil for further development.

Did you know that…

... oaks were considered property of the state in Sweden until around 1830, when ownership was transferred to the landowner? It was Gustav Vasa, who in 1558 established the king's oak trees. He needed the wood for ship construction.

... the penalty for wrongful felling or harming of an oak in Sweden in 1810 was a heavy fine or a month's imprisonment on bread and water?

There is certainly a limit to how old a tree might be, but the limit varies for many reasons. The age limit is dependent on which tree species is in question, how it grows, and especially where it grows. In Sweden the Rumskulla oak, the enormous giant oak tree that stands in Northern Kvill in Småland, is considered to be the oldest tree in the country at more than 1,000 years old. In California, in the United States, the sequoia trees are said to grow to be nearly 4,000 years old.

Why don't trees on slopes grow at a slant?

Tree sprouts (as well as other sprouts) always grow upward and the roots grow downward. If the plant's location is disturbed, so that it is horizontal for example, the plant will curve as needed to grow vertically/upward with the root growing downward. These curvature movements, called geotropism, represent the plant's reaction to Earth's gravity. As with phototropism, it is the question of the reaction of a growing body to a unilaterally acting force.

Why are leaves such bright colors in the fall?

Throughout the summer, leaves are green, but before abscission the green chlorophyll breaks down. Colors then appear, dependent upon natural dyes, such as carotenoids and anthocyanins. In the autumn, most trees have leaves that are mainly in a yellow or amber tint. Maple, and often rowan and aspen, are known for their varied red color scale.

The yellow color comes from carotenoids found in the leaf all summer, but that have been masked by chlorophyll. (Carotenoids give the carrot its color.) The red color tones come primarily from anthocyanins, which are created the fall. In cell cavities (vacuoles), sugar formed during the day is converted to anthocyanins, especially during cold nights. Anthocyanin formation intensity varies from year to year and is likely influenced primarily by temperature.

Any biological function of the bright colors is not yet clear. Possibly, the strong autumn colors relate to a number of interacting factors that may have important functions for various plant physiological processes (such as varying efficiency in the recycling of nutrient resources, like nitrogen and phosphorus), and which vary in importance between different species and geographic areas. It has also been suggested that the autumn colors are a result of coevolution between insects and plants.

And then they fall

In trees, leaves grow old and die practically simultaneously. It seems to be mainly the shorter days (or daylight length, known as photoperiod), but also the temperature that triggers plants' winter preparedness. Abscission can be interpreted as an adaptation to the water and cold that characterize the winter in many climates. In birch and several other trees, it is the leaf that takes up the photoperiodic signal. The actual leaf falling is made possible by an abscission layer formed at the leaf base and attached to the trunk. When the middle lamella, and to some extent the cell wall, becomes slimy and dissolves, abscission layer cells detach easily from each other. Various internal and external factors determine when this layer will be dissolved and the leaf will come loose from its mounting.

Did you know that...

... alder leaves are still green when they fall off? This may be because the leaves contain high amounts of mineral nutrients, such as nitrogen, that are in short supply in many other trees.

193

BERRIES, NUTS, FRUIT?

What about the onion makes people cry?

Short answer: It's allicin.

A little longer of an answer: When the onion is crushed, the enzyme alliinase combines with the compound alliin, which in turn condenses into allicin. This anti-bacterial substance found in yellow and white onions tastes strong and makes the eyes fill with tears. Its proper function is to protect the bulb from insects.

What is the difference between berries and fruit?

An orange is a fruit and a blueberry is a berry. So far, it sounds easy. But where is the line between fruit and berries? The botanical definition of a fruit says that a fruit is a mature ovary and its contents. According to this definition, the core of an apple houses the real fruit, as do the small seeds on the outside of a strawberry. A fruit is thus parts of the flower formed to help propagation take place.

For the botanist, a berry is a juicy fruit, often with many seeds, but sometimes even with a single seed (e.g., the barberry). Berries must also be deciduous and never open. Therefore, tomato, cucumber, and melon are more berries than strawberries and raspberries.

Berries, in everyday life, are categorized in the fruit department—namely fruits that are so small that you can pop a lot of them in your mouth simultaneously.

STONE FRUIT AND ACCESSORY FRUIT

A *stone fruit* is a juicy fruit with a seed surrounded by a hard shell. These include cherries, sloes, and plums.

In an *accessory fruit*, the small seeds in the juicy tissue are the real fruits. Examples are rosehips, rowanberries, apples, and many more.

Aggregate fruits are raspberries, blackberries, cloudberries, etc.

Everything that we commonly refer to as a berry is not a real berry. In the older literature, the suffix "berry" was added to the end, and in many cases—strawberries, raspberries, cranberries—the ending is still there.

Then we have the concepts of fruits and vegetables. Fruit, as we see, can be botanically verified and classified, but for vegetables, there is no scientific definition. What we describe as a vegetable is usually determined by our eating habits. Vegetables can, botanically speaking, be roots, stems, leaves, flowers, and in some cases even fruits. There are numerous examples of fruits (in the botanical sense) called vegetables. These include peppers, where the name reveals its botanical origin, but also beans, cucumbers, tomatoes, squash, and eggplant.

What is a nut?

Nuts are a division of plants that are characterized as fruits! They are dry and contain one seed. They do not open when they are ripe, but the whole fruit spreads and opens only when the seed is ready to germinate.

Sometimes nuts have wings, like those of the birch, or florets, like dandelions, allowing wind spread. Some nuts have barbs, which allow them to cling to animal fur. Some things that are commonly called nuts, such as coconuts and walnuts, are not nuts in the botanical sense.

Relax, do not worry: birds will not choke and there is no risk that grains will swell in their stomachs. It is a myth that it is dangerous for birds if you throw rice at a bride and groom.

Birds that eat large seeds, like grains of rice, are designed for it. Why would birds like the yellowhammer be able to eat whole grains if they would be harmed by them? Put some uncooked rice in water and see what happens. If left long enough, the grains may swell a little bit, but the turnover time of the birds' digestive/intestinal tract is so short that it does not pose a danger to them. The birds themselves know what and how much they can eat.

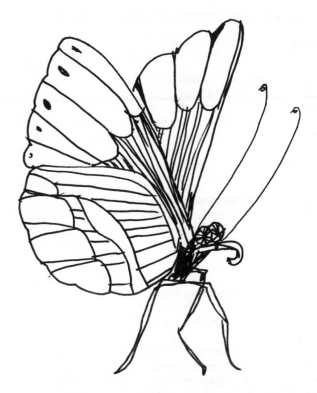

Why are meadows important?

Butterflies fluttering over a flourishing meadow are part of many people's idea of what a summer must contain.

But today there are few meadows left, and not many butterflies. In Sweden, natural grassland is only along the shoreline, where the winter ice cuts off all nearby vegetation so no trees or shrubs can grow. All other meadows are created by man and depend on a grazing workforce. Many species labeled "abundant" in the butterfly books of 50 years ago are now endangered and at risk of dying out.

In modern agriculture and forestry, there is no room for meadows, they claim, leading to the disappearance of important habitats and thus many butterflies and other insects that live there. The few wild flowers that remain are driven out, often by grass, which leads to the caterpillars and other insects having nothing to live by. This in turn leads to a reduction in availability of food for the birds, and in the end we humans can suffer.

Other open lands that are important butterfly and insect habitats that you might not consider are electricity and telephone line corridors, as well as military training and firing grounds. Practice fields are like the environments that flowers and insects have adapted to over thousands of years: no fertilizer to boost growth, and heavy vehicles tearing up the ground and soil in spots where new species are given the opportunity to establish themselves. Similarly, mammoths and aurochs (the ancient ancestor of domestic cattle) roamed the earth long ago, and the same effect was found in small-scale agriculture that existed until the '50s. In many places there is higher biodiversity in

201

military firing fields than in the nature reserves next door. Firing ranges are the absolute last habitats of many endangered species, but they may be on the way out. So are electricity and telecommunications corridors as we increasingly bury the lines.

New butterflies that arrive in these areas—and there are some!—are generalists, meaning they do not specialize in certain areas or certain foods. These butterflies feed on dandelions and nettles, plants that benefit from human progress.

WHAT TO DO?

But there are opportunities. Motocross- and racetracks with cars and motorcycles that tear up the soil are extremely important for many insect species. Old quarries that are warm and open are also good. Therefore, it is important to preserve these and not plant again or cover them with topsoil and grass.

Another important habitat for butterflies is the ditch bank. Many of these are now maintained by farmers who formerly managed meadows. This requires cutting the edges quite late in the summer, in August or September, when the flowers have blossomed and gone to seed, and the insects have begun to prepare for the winter. To avoid grasses taking over, it is better to remove the clippings rather than allow them to remain as fertilizer.

Oases of butterflies can be created almost anywhere. Another example is the golf course fairway. There could be spaces created for butterflies and birds simply by combining meadow flowers with ponds.

Another way to help environmental conservation is to look after the butterflies that are around us. In Sweden, we still do not even know all of the butterflies that live in the islands in our archipelago or in large parts of northern Sweden.

With the help of a good guide it is, for the most part, pretty easy to recognize most butterflies. You can self-report the butterflies you find to a local entomological center, or, in Sweden, preferably to the Species Information Centre at the Swedish University of Agricultural Sciences.

Butterflies are also a very good indicator of the status of the environment. When they disappear, we know that something is about to happen.

Did you know that...

... nature is just waiting for you to come and visit?
So pack your backpack—don't forget binoculars and a
magnifying glass—and go!